Images in Sand

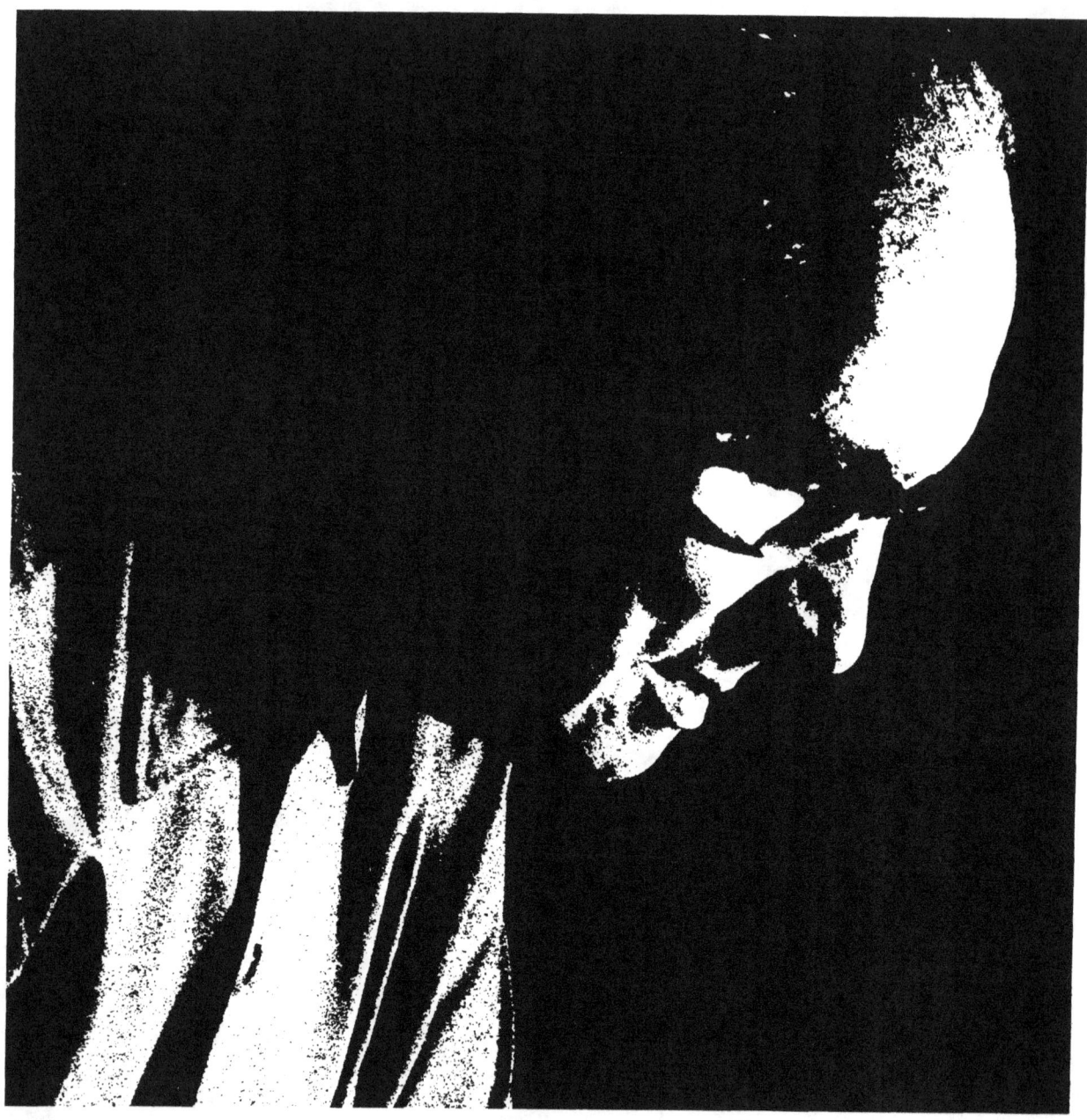

Janis Sternbergs
IMAGES IN SAND

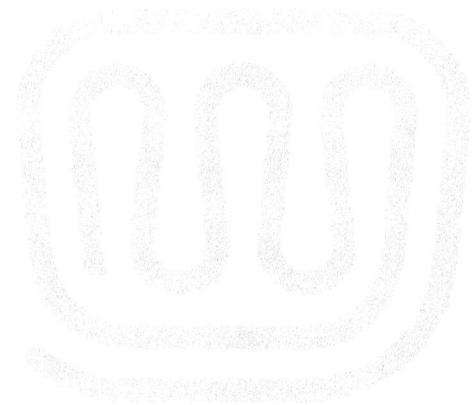

The University Press of Kentucky

ISBN: 978-0-8131-5492-3

Library of Congress Catalog Card Number: 76-46030
Copyright © 1977 by The University Press of Kentucky

A statewide cooperative scholarly publishing agency
serving Berea College, Centre College of Kentucky,
Eastern Kentucky University, The Filson Club,
Georgetown College, Kentucky Historical Society,
Kentucky State University, Morehead State University,
Murray State University, Northern Kentucky University,
Transylvania University, University of Kentucky,
University of Louisville, and Western Kentucky University.

Editorial and Sales Offices: Lexington, Kentucky 40506

For my wife, Erika, with love

Contents

Preface

Sand is a fascinating medium, but a work of art produced in sand is fragile and cannot be preserved except through photography. Many beautiful works of art have perished from the insensitivity of man or the turbulence of nature. Most of the treasures of the ancient world are gone, as are the sound waves of great musical performances of past centuries. But today technology can to some degree preserve the essence of the original in the arts, and so it is with sand sculptures. The photograph becomes the record of what would otherwise have perished. The fragility of an image made in sand prohibits its preservation in any other way. Even a slight puff of breath upon the sand disturbs the particles. I have tried spraying various fixatives over the sandy surfaces, but a minute drop of fixative lands on one grain of sand and attracts the grains around it so that the surface becomes coarse and the image loses its original quality. Consequently, a photographic record becomes the only means of preserving the original image.

In creating sand sculptures I have observed that preconceived visual ideas are hard to work out and imitation of natural forms is difficult; but for spontaneous creative work, sand is an excellent material. It immediately and dramatically responds to the artist's movements, encouraging him to experiment with different techniques and tools. A creative mind sees ways to use the new visual effects thus produced. Every time I "play" with the sand I make new discoveries in the behavior of this medium. I have experimented with many sandlike substances, including salt and seeds, but aluminum oxide grains, because of their uniform size and comparatively heavy molecular weight, produce the most satisfying results. The particles tend to stay where they are placed, which makes for crisp sculptural edges. I use the sand dry, because in this state it lends itself more readily to shifting when I am forming the images.

As in spontaneous work in any other medium, the first movement an artist makes tends to dictate all subsequent steps, and only the artist's instinct tells him when the creation is complete. While specific images may be created intentionally—or appear spontaneously in the sand—it is good to get away from recognizable objects so that one can see the beauty of shapes and forms in their purer states. Particular visual effects in the compositions presented here are usually the results of deliberate experimentation, but occasionally they have evolved by accident. One day when I was about to destroy a completed image, I lifted one side of the sheet of cardboard I was working on and the sand shifted, creating a new visual effect in the imagery. On another occasion taps on the table caused the sand to move into a new pattern formation, and repeated blows caused a kind of "clotting" effect in the sand.

Once the image is completed, I photograph it. In photographing artworks of this type the lighting is critical. Too much light on any sculpture destroys the image, for we see sculpture largely in terms of the play of light and shadow. If a light is placed directly above the working area, the sand image gets lost. Experimentation with the lighting on each image is necessary for discovery of the best vantage point.

I did not remain entirely satisfied with the photographs as records of the images, and it soon occurred to me that by use of photo-screen process printing I could add color effects and produce works in an art form in which I have long been interested.

From the black-and-white photographs I prepared screened 4-by-5-inch negatives, using (positive) Kodak Magenta Contact Screen in a conventional square-dot 200-line-per-inch ruling. When this negative is enlarged to 16 by 20 inches on graphic film, it gives a positive with a dot size suitable for screen printing. (Detailed description of the use of contact screens and preparation of printing stencils can be found in Kodak information brochures as well as in such works as Albert Kosloff's "Photographic Screen Process Printing," 4th ed. [Cincinnati, Ohio: Signs of the Times Publishing Co., 1972].) For a rich effect I print first with a light hue, then shift the register very slightly to the left or right and print from the same stencil once more, this time with a harmonious darker hue. Another method is to print the first time with either a light or a dark hue from an unscreened positive. In this method if a dark hue is used in the first printing, the second print is made with a negative stencil and opaque light ink.

A selection of twenty 11-by-14-inch black-and-white photographs of my works in sand was displayed in my "Retrospective Exhibit" in the art gallery of the University of Kentucky, October 12–November 9, 1969. (In the catalog they were described as "Photographic Records of Perishable Objects in Sand.") Twenty new photographs were added in my one-man exhibit in the art gallery of the Lexington Art League, Lexington, Kentucky, February 7–March 6, 1971. A traveling exhibition of the color prints, sponsored by the Kentucky Art Commission, opened October 5, 1975, in Louisville and is to tour the state for two years.

I should like to thank all those who have knowingly and unknowingly contributed to the idea of this book based on the results of my experimentation with sand and sandlike substances as a medium for creative art. I am especially grateful to two friends and former students—Elsie Kennedy and Jim Foose.

Introduction

In their search for means of creating visual imagery, artists occasionally develop new techniques by deliberately pursuing them, while at other times such innovations appear more or less by accident. In 1798, for want of a scrap of paper, Aloys Senefelder wrote his mother's laundry list with the first materials that came to hand in his printmaking studio—greasy ink on a smooth stone. This was the beginning of lithography. In 1965 Janis Sternbergs, while working with intaglio prints, made a few playful lines in a pile of sand on his studio table and was struck by the unusual confluence of shadows he had created. So began his series of images in sand.

Of course, neither lithography nor sand images made their advent into the arts as fully developed concepts. Like an individual work of art, a new art form begins as an idea and "grows," urged on by the creative curiosity of the artist. The perpetual question in the creative mind is "What would happen if . . . ?" To answer that question requires a wealth of time and energy spent in exploring and experimenting, and the answer may well turn out to be a mere novelty, soon abandoned by serious artists. Yet sometimes an idea will result in a new art form that not only has genuine artistic value, but can inspire other artists to new and greater passages in their own work.

The purpose of this book is to share and to perpetuate a new concept in the visual arts. Sand images are not only aesthetically satisfying in themselves; the concept readily lends itself to exploration in photography, printmaking, ceramics, and other areas of art where surfaces may be covered with light-sensitive emulsions and made receptive to photographic imagery.

Sand is commonly found in the studios of artists and craftsmen, for it is a useful and versatile material. It is an abrasive. Mixed with paint, it gives texture to paintings. It is used in casting and in making glazes for pottery and enamels for metalwork. In 1965 Janis Sternbergs was developing a method of forming images for intaglio prints with whiting, watery gelatin, and sand, a combination that gives aquatint-like effects. During this period of experimentation he idly drew some lines in a pile of sand on a table near his working area. He was taken with the image and made a photograph of the sand pile. The resulting photographic print had the appearance of a great earth sculpture of vast depth and breadth. This whetted his appetite for further experimentation with the medium— creating sand images and photographing the results—and his exploration has continued to the present time.

The illusion of sculptural qualities that can be created with sand, combined with the different textural effects that can be produced in the images, could serve as an almost endless source of fresh inspiration for both the amateur and the professional photographer. Motion picture and television photographers might enlarge sand imagery to monumental proportions for use as backdrops of either a realistic or an imaginary nature. It is not inconceivable that an entire film could be made using nothing except sand imagery—either as a form of animation or as a new sensation in visual experiences.

In the area of printmaking, the images can be enlarged or reduced and then transferred onto a light-sensitive silk screen stencil—or onto etching or lithographic plates that have been treated with a light-sensitive emulsion.

Sand imagery would also lend itself readily to textile design. In fact, the utilitarian application of this process is limited only by the imagination of those who wish to adopt the techniques and apply them to various fields.

The effectiveness of these sand images in stimulating aesthetic response depends, of course, upon the quality of the entire composition. To achieve his results, Janis Sternbergs has drawn upon his many areas of knowledge and creative ability—his skill as a graphic artist, his sense of design, his feeling for the material. The plates included in this book not only suggest the range and potential of sand as a medium of expression in the visual arts, but attest as well to the imagination and versatility of the artist.

Elsie Kennedy

The first section of this book provides an illustrated guide to Sternbergs's methods of working with sand. There has been no intention of prescribing exact equipment or listing all suitable tools; the artist's imagination will encourage him to experiment with many different implements and techniques as he becomes familiar with the possibilities of the medium.

The second part of the book is a catalog
containing 154 photographs of sand images, the
first 16 reproduced in color by a process similar
to the one the artist himself uses. Through the
catalog one can come to realize the variety and
power of Sternbergs's images in sand.

Some Ways to Work in Sand

Plate 1 (opposite) My basic equipment consists of an eighth-inch Masonite plate measuring about thirteen by nineteen inches, a jar of sand (Type W aluminum oxide grain, grit 220, available from the Carborundum Company, Niagara Falls, New York, and at many machinery supply and lithographic supply firms) and various tools and other objects for drawing in the sand and creating textures. On the Masonite base lay a slightly smaller sheet of light card stock, about the same color value as the sand, or darker. Pour a little sand onto the cardboard or sprinkle it from a jar through a piece of silk stretched over the opening. For a good view of the work as it is in progress, a lamp — preferably a high-intensity reading lamp — is placed on the work table with the bulb only slightly higher than the work surface.

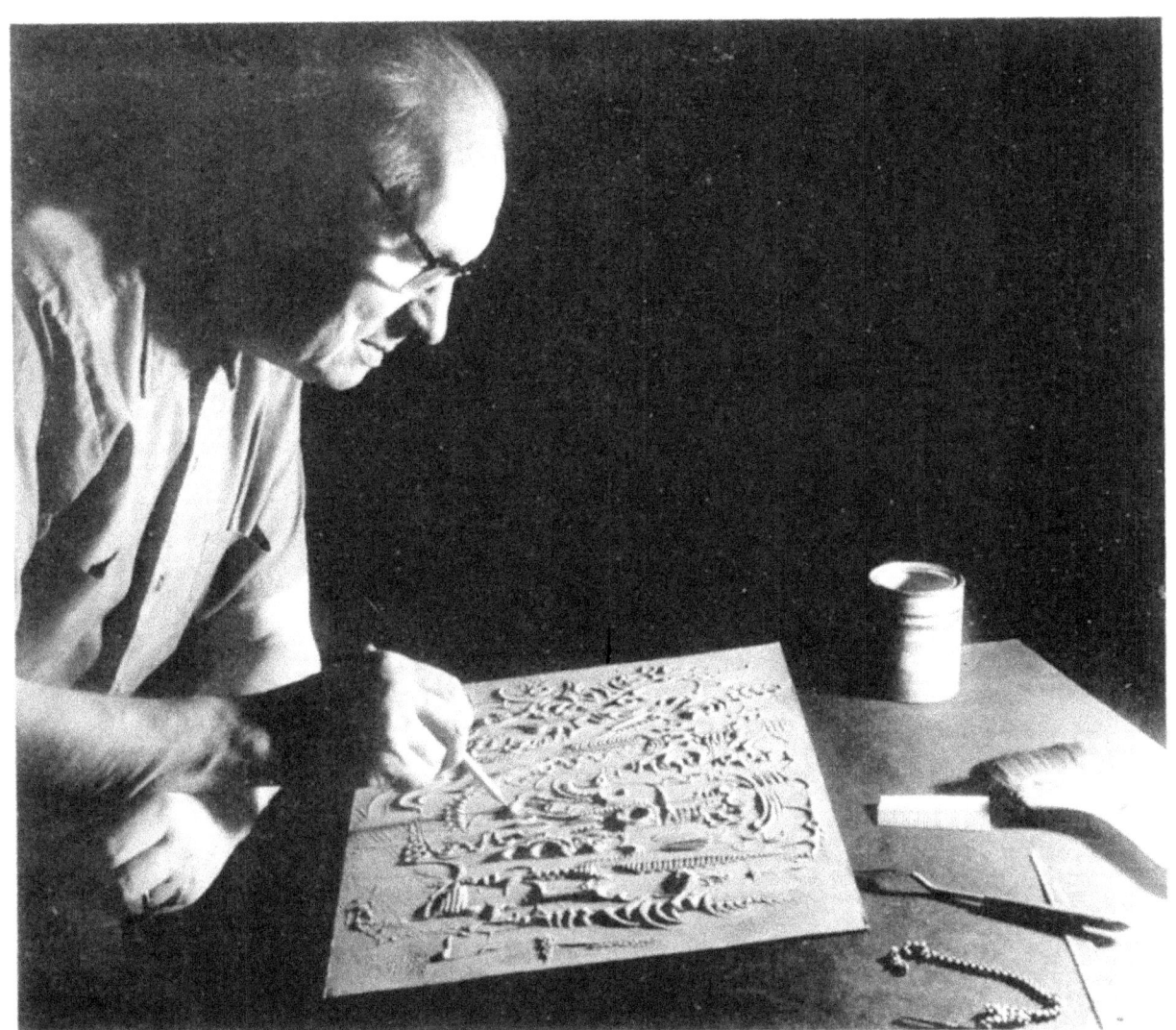

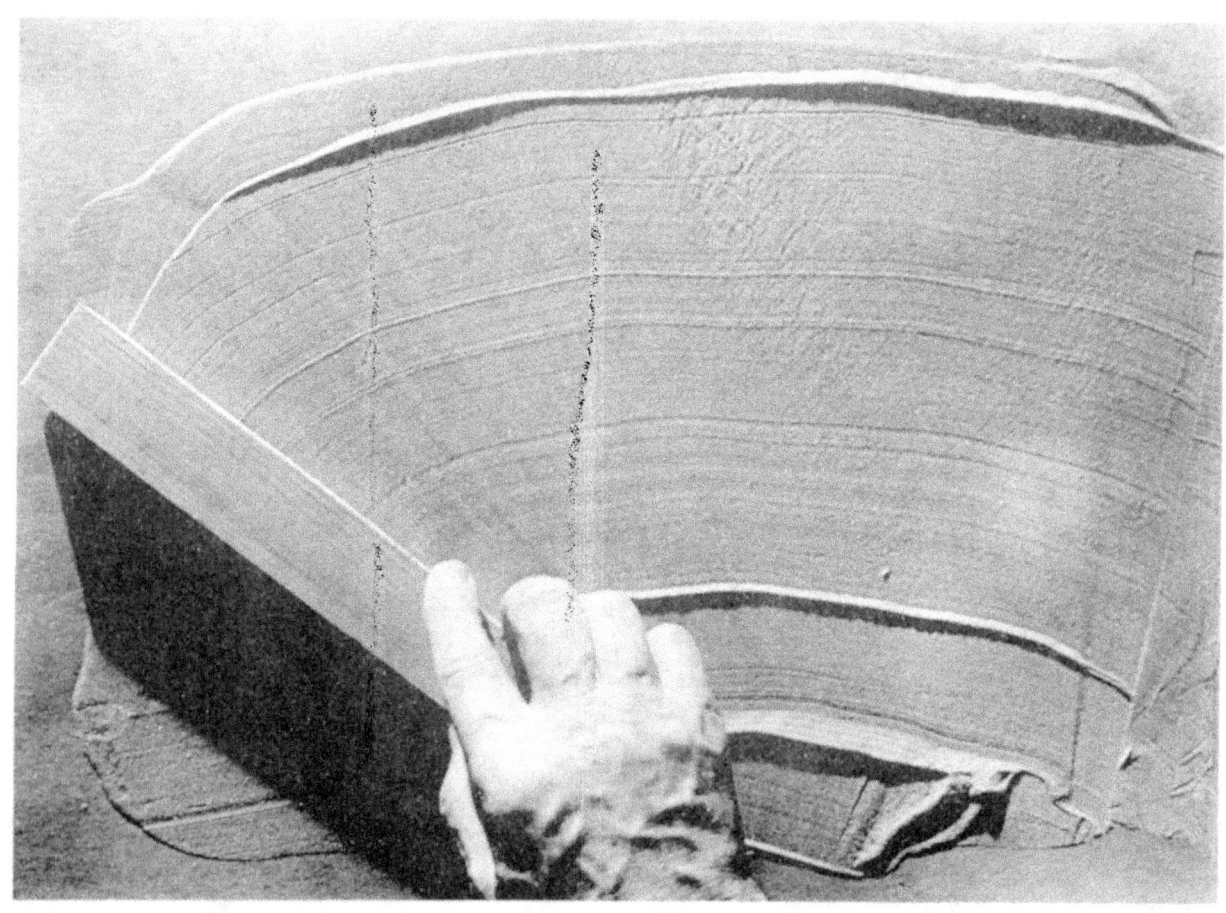

Plate 2 The first step is to flatten, smooth out, and spread the sand, creating background texture.

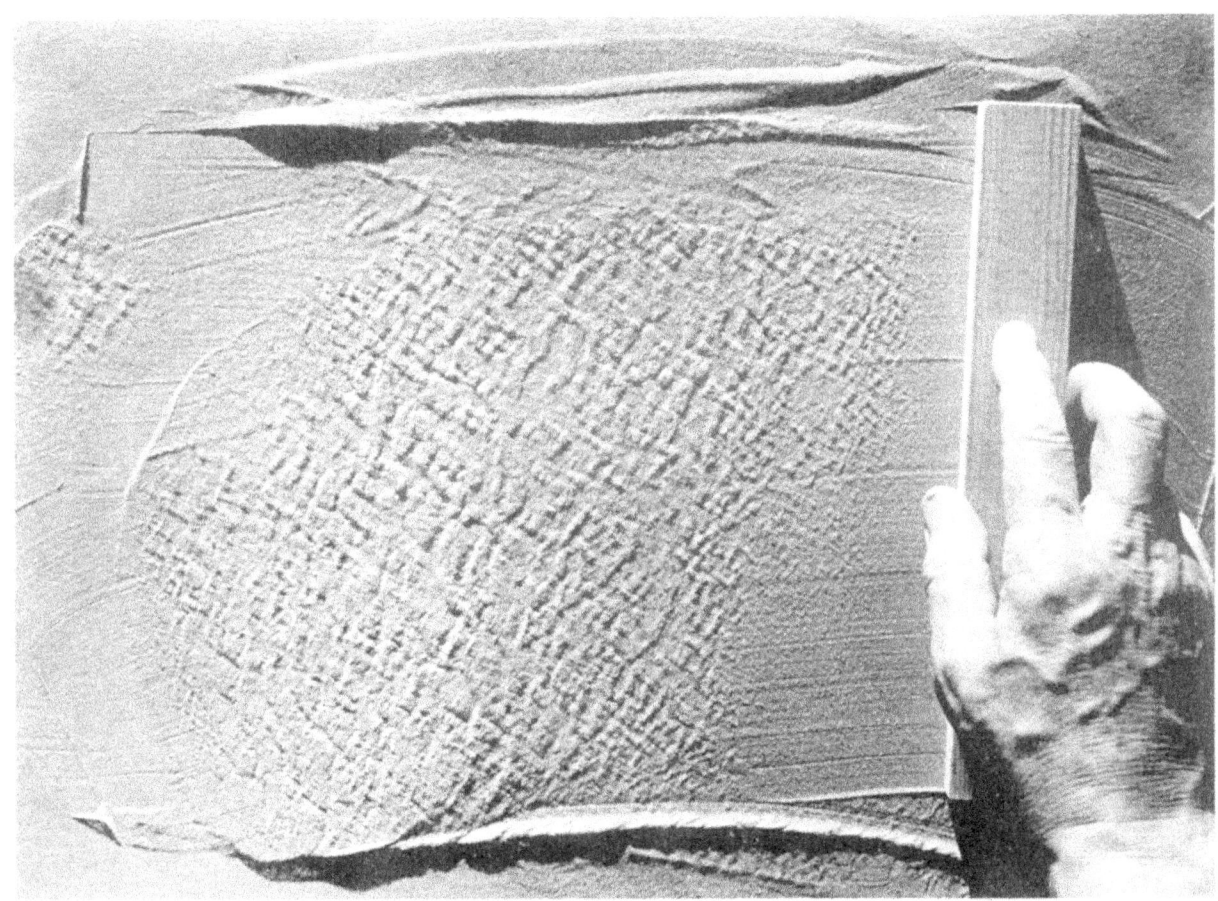

Plate 3 A quick sweep with a small board will produce ripples in the sand.

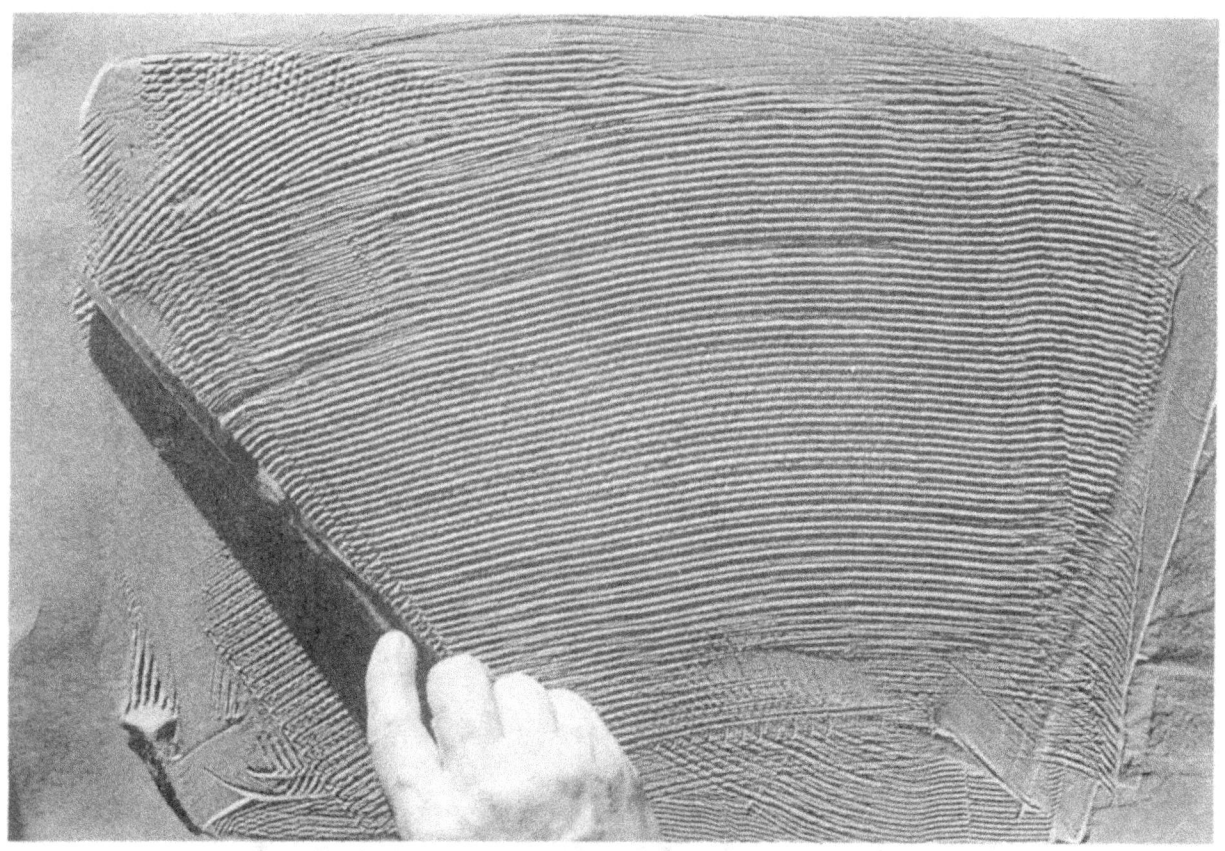

Plate 4 A saw blade can be used to produce a textured layer of sand of a uniform thickness.

Plate 5 (opposite) Designs may incorporate the saw blade texture or use it as a background. (*Image CXI*)

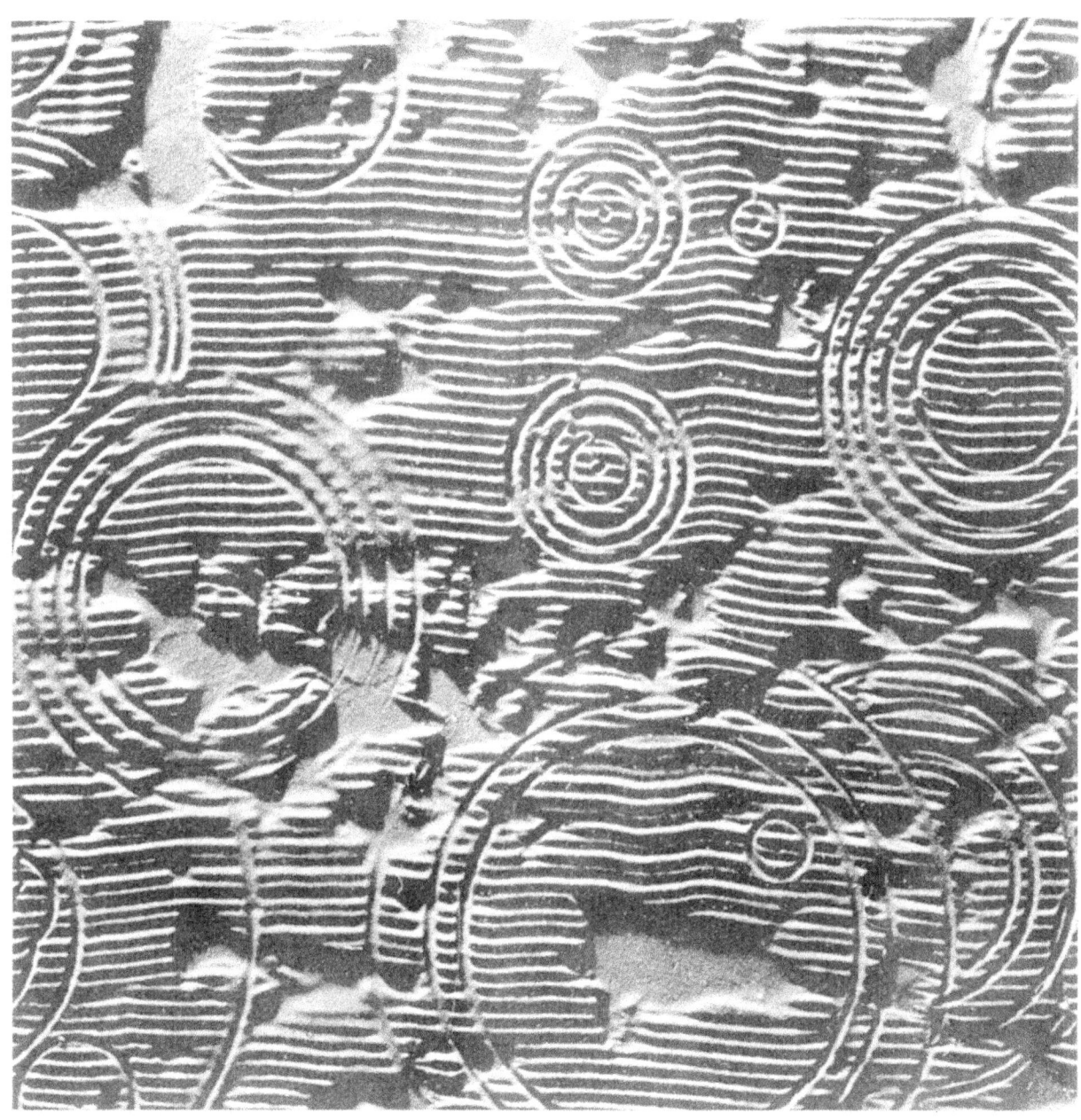

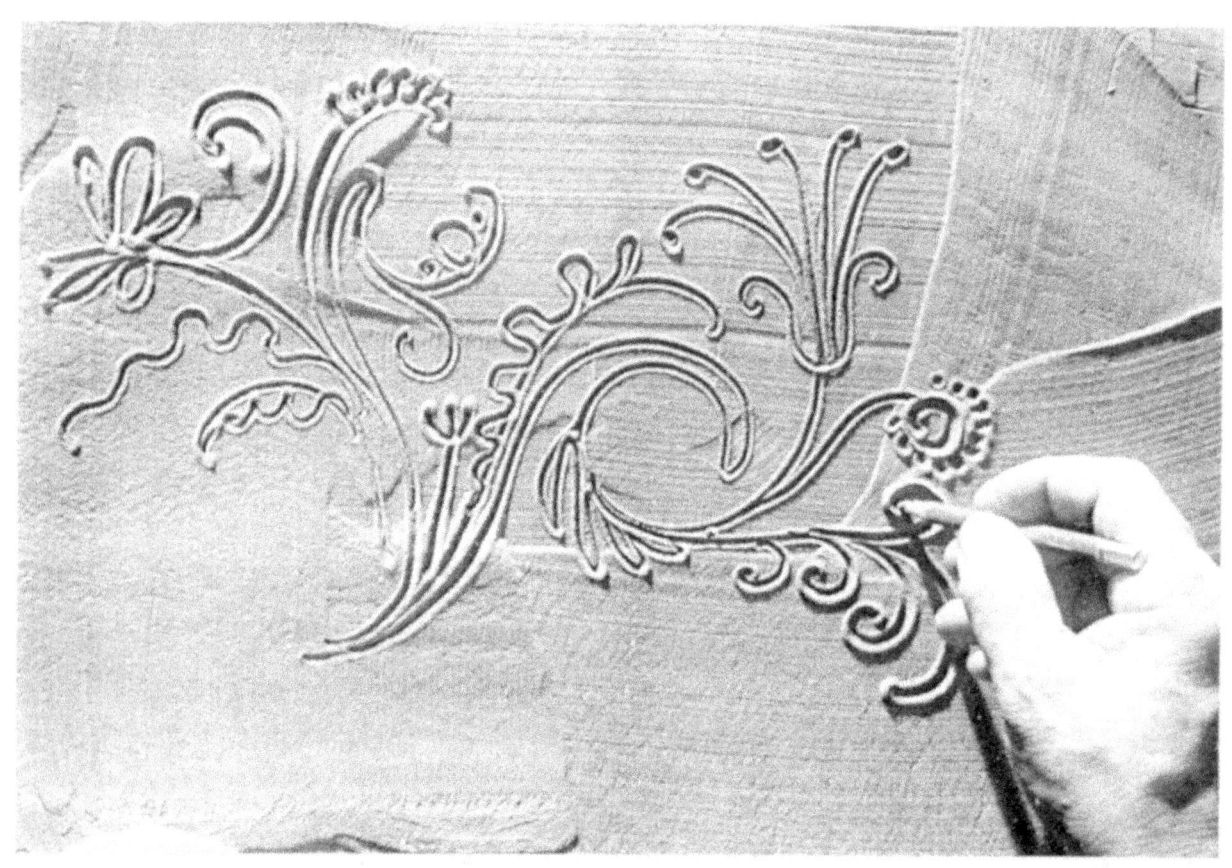

Plate 6 Any pointed tool can be used for drawing — a stick, pencil, or needle.

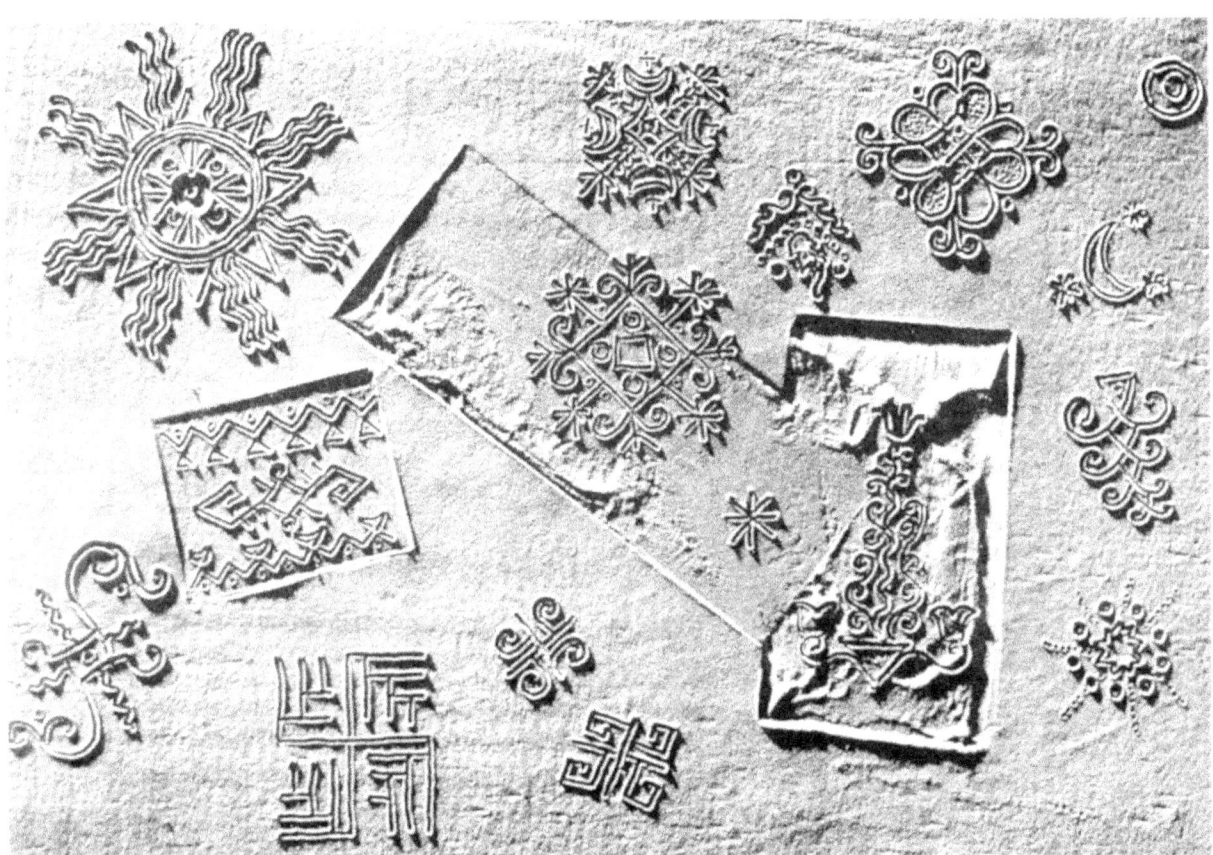

Plate 7 After smoothing the background with a ruler and then pressing a small piece of wood into the sand to create indentations, I did the drawing with a blunt-pointed pencil. If the lead is broken out of the pencil, it will not leave marks on the cardboard.
(*Image CLXXI*)

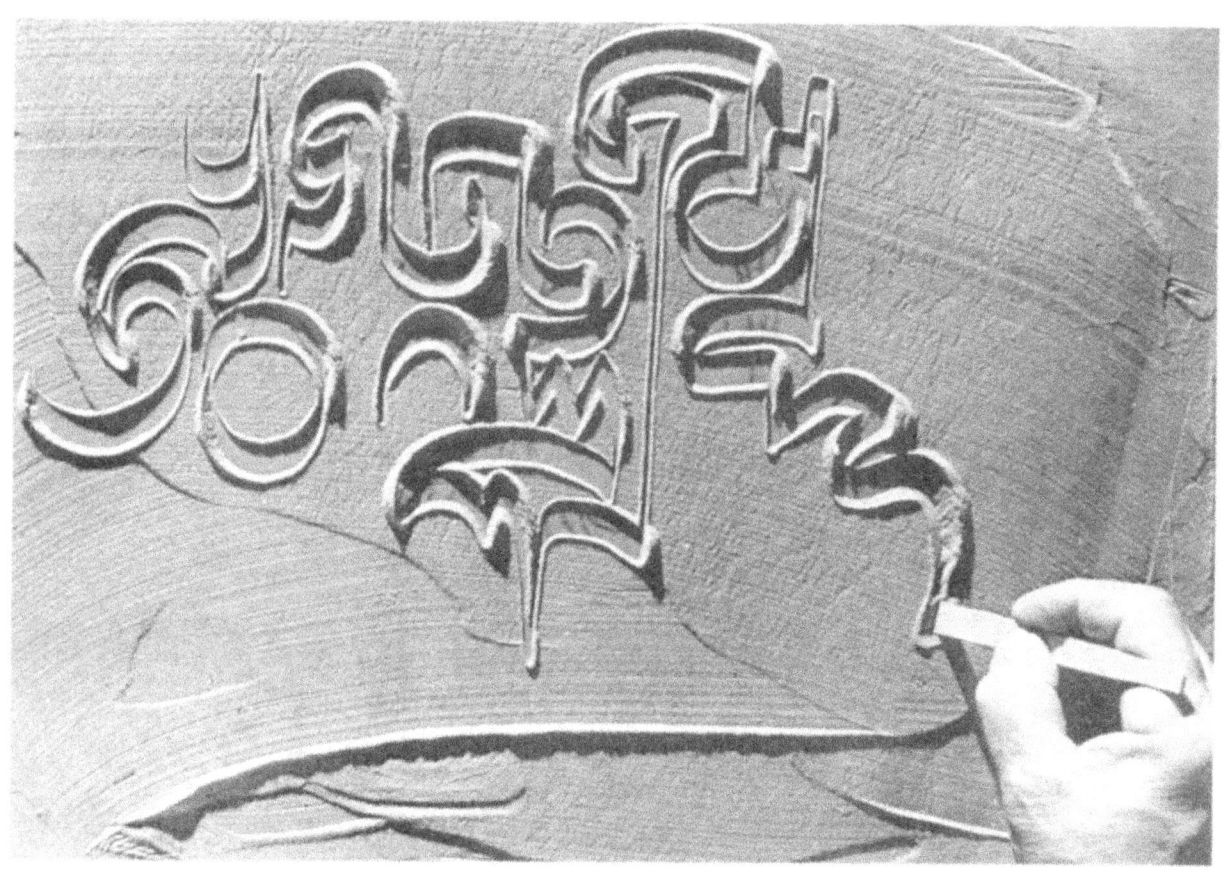

Plate 8 and Plate 9 (opposite) For calligraphy, use a chisel point. **(Plate 9: *Image CVI*)**

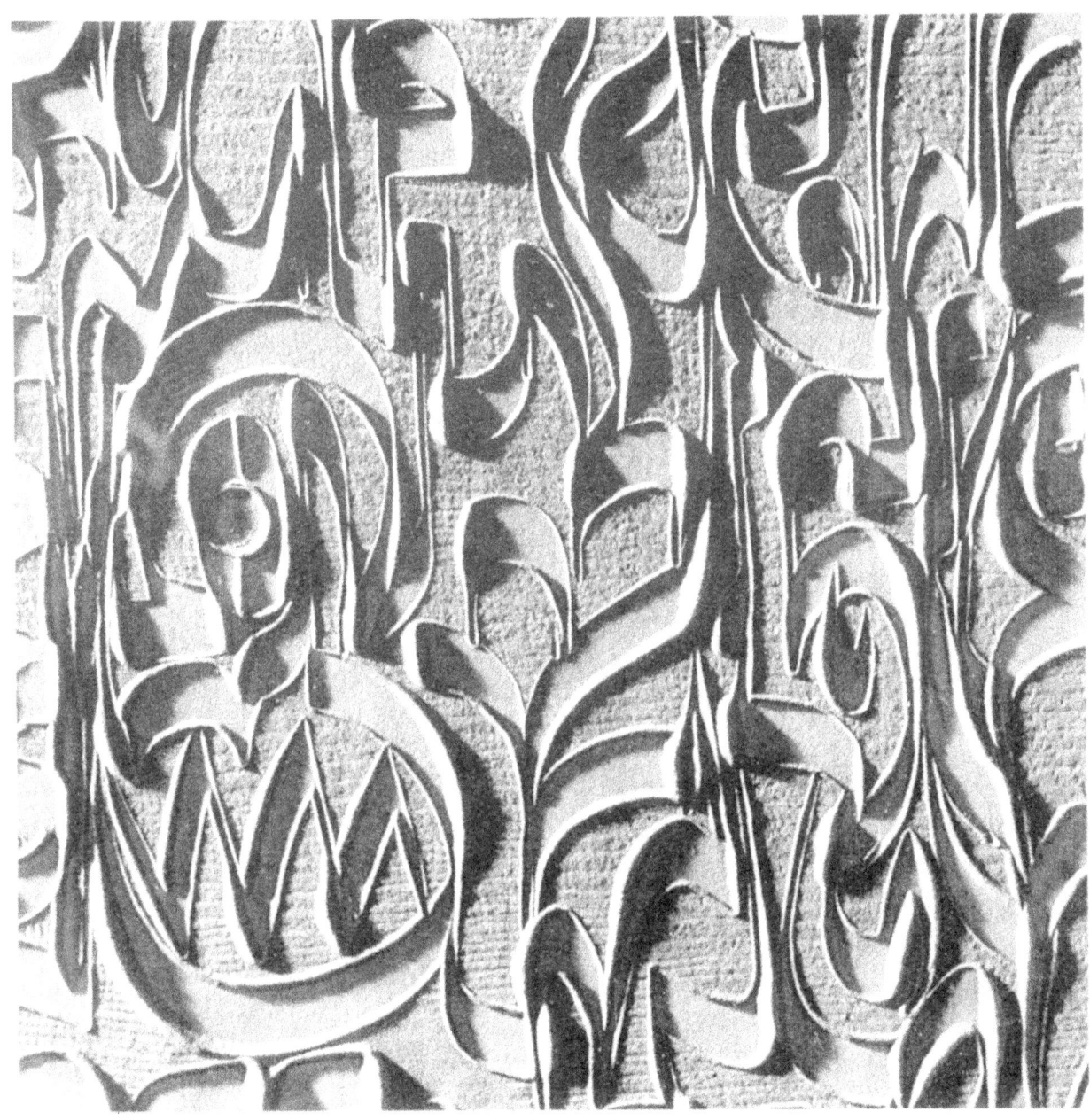

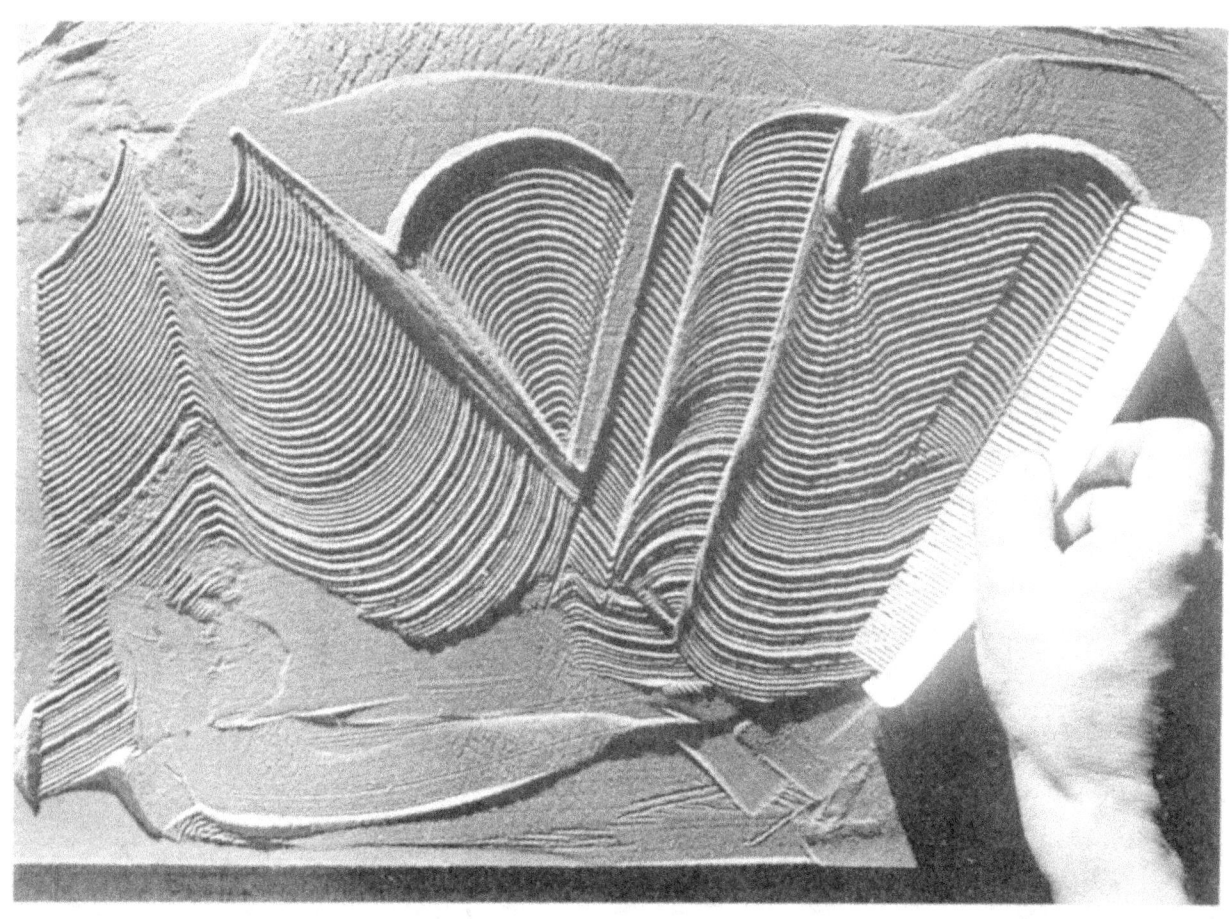

Plate 10 A comb can be used to create visually exciting patterns.

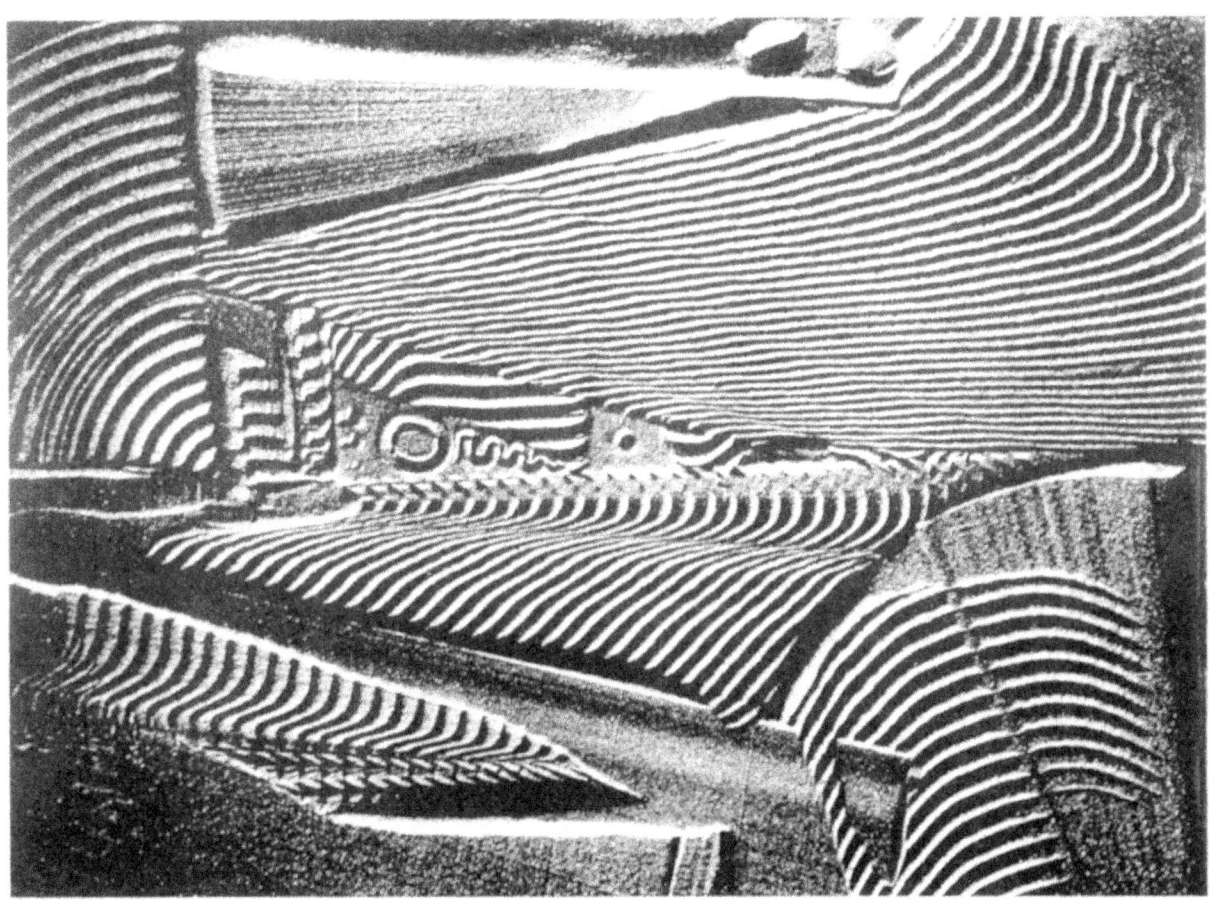

Plate 11 An image like this one depends for its illusion of vastness upon the location and intensity of the light source when it is being photographed. (*Image XI: Stadium*)

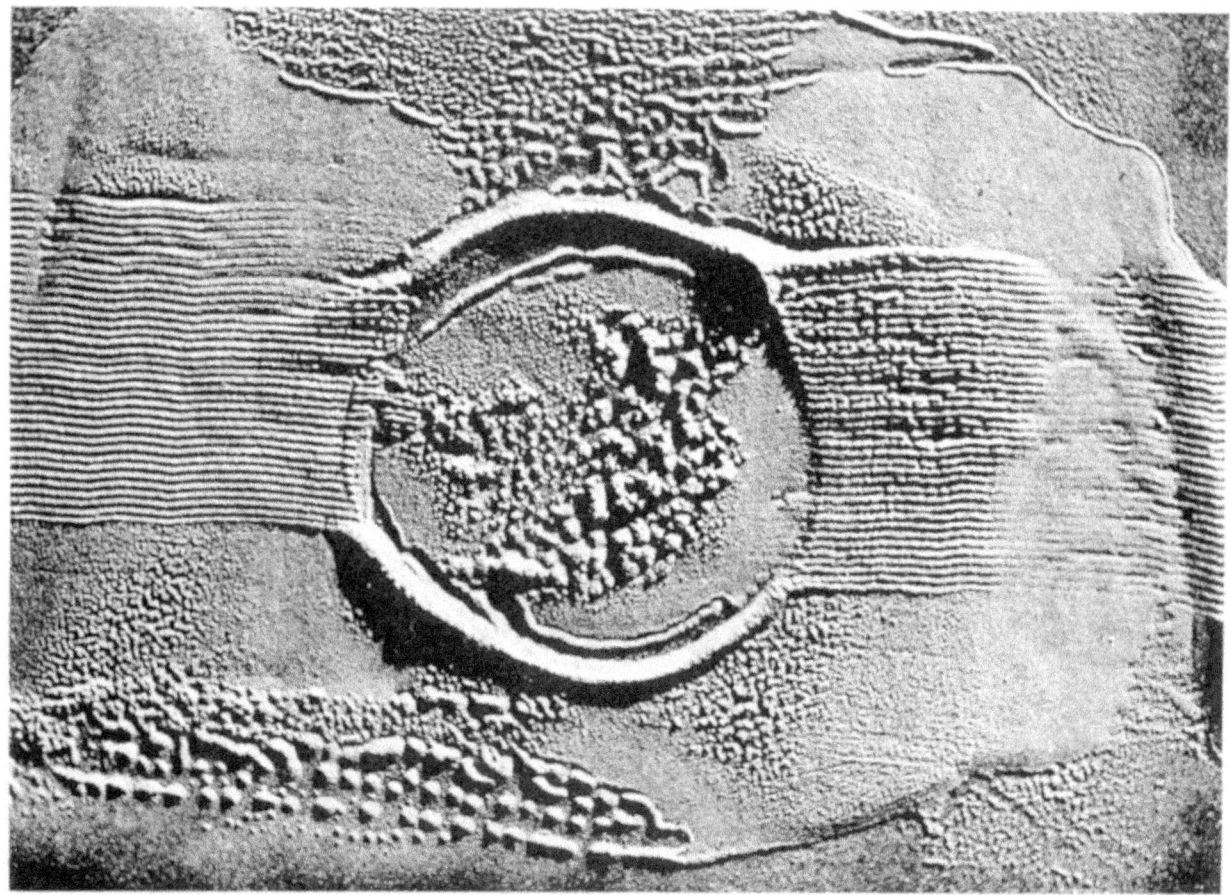

Plate 12 Various tools and techniques can be combined.
As I worked with the different tools and methods
available to me, my images began to take on a sculptural
appearance. Tapping the bottom of the table produced
the pebbling. (*Image LX: Crater*)

Plate 13 (opposite) The highs and lows were created
first, with a flat piece of wood; then a spool of nylon
cord was rolled over all levels. (*Image XII*)

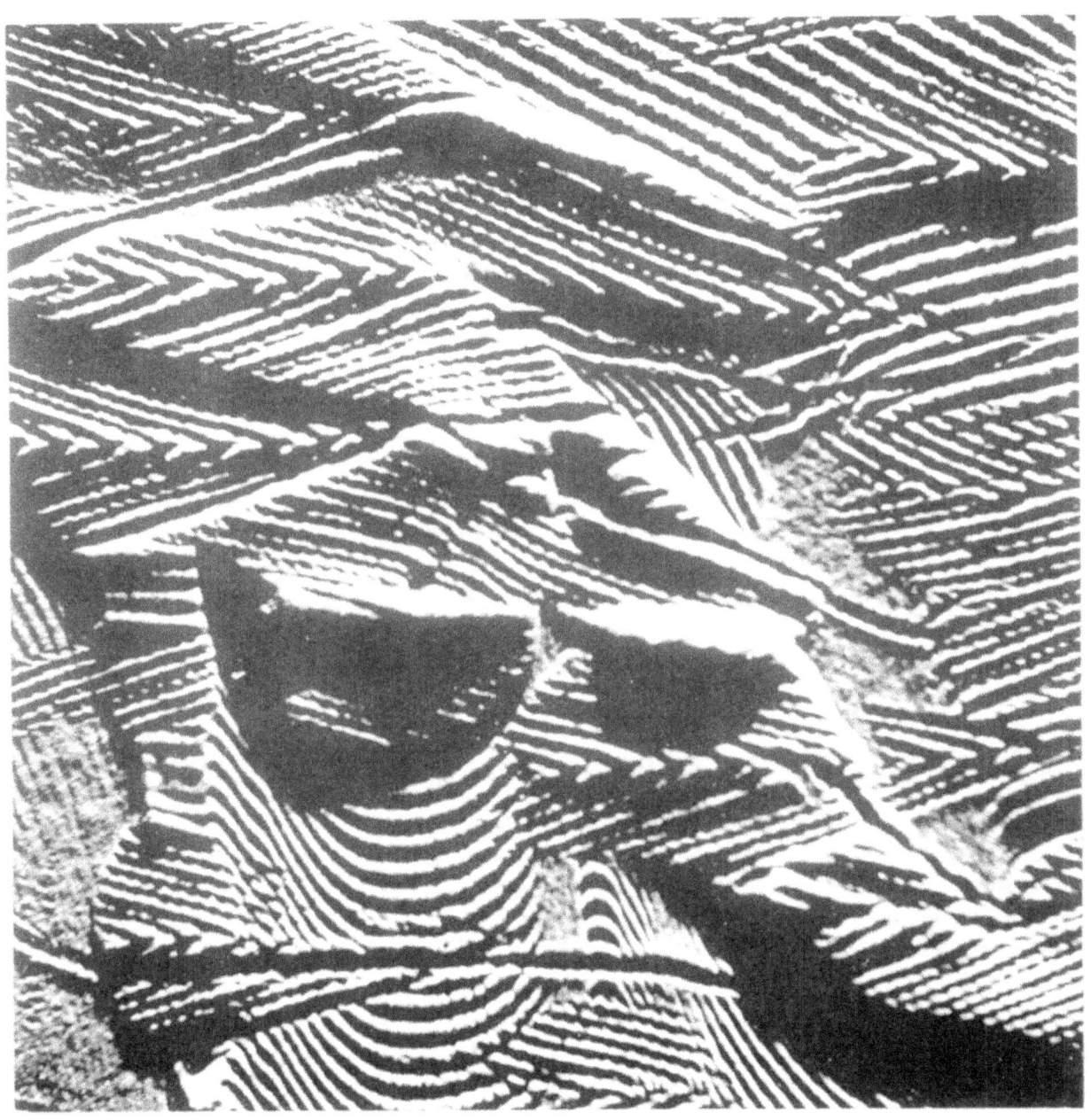

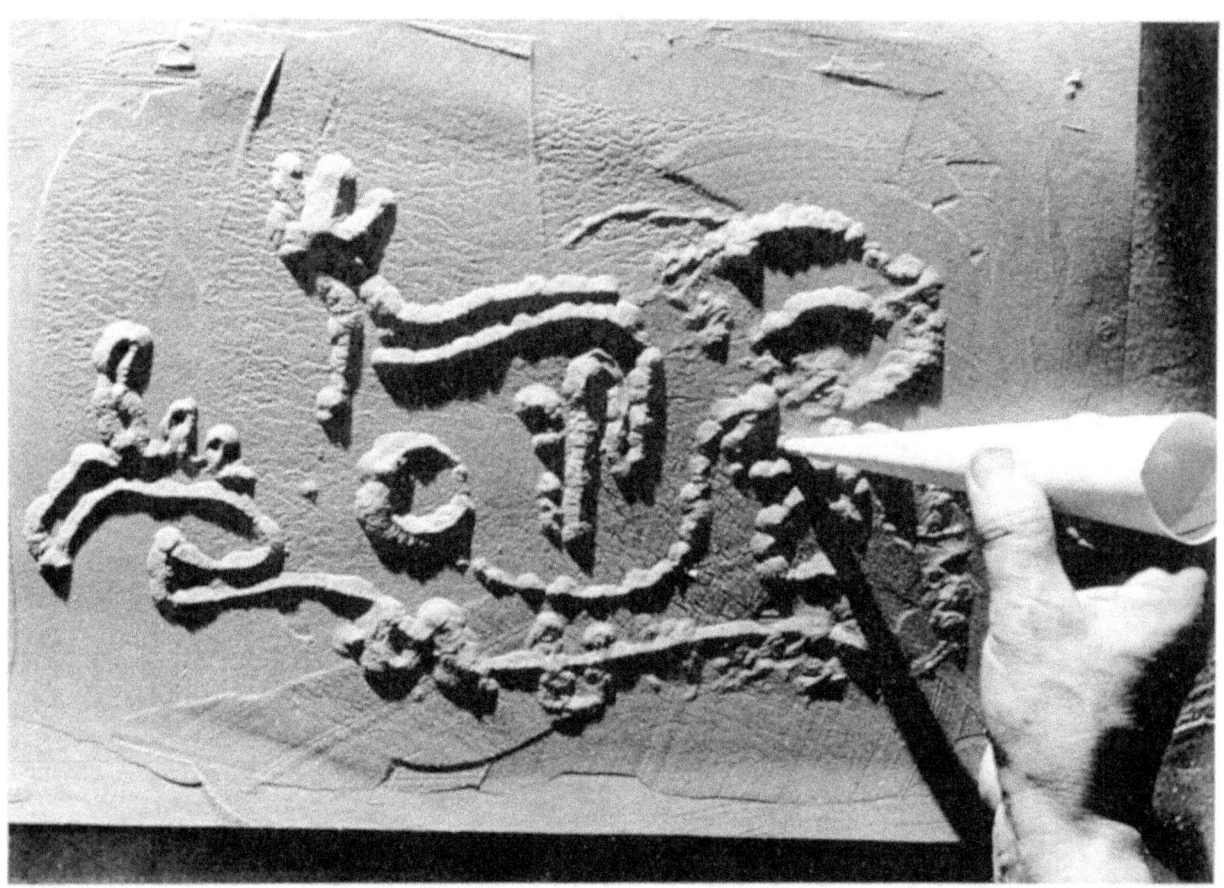

Plate 14 and Plate 15 (opposite) Sand deposed through
a funnel creates raised, flattened shapes; it is a little like
pressing ornaments onto a cake from an icing gun. **(Plate
15:** *Image CXXXII*)

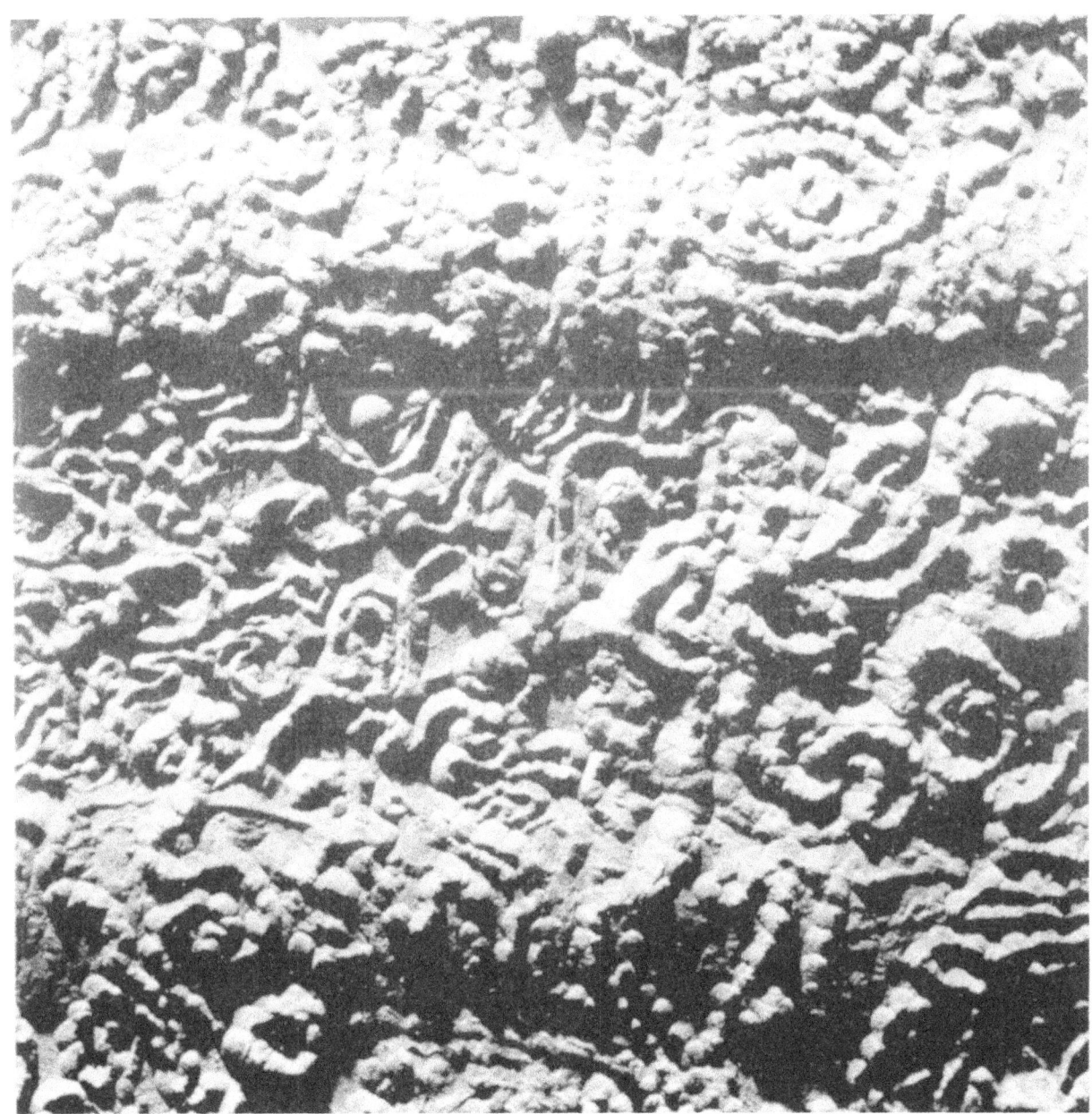

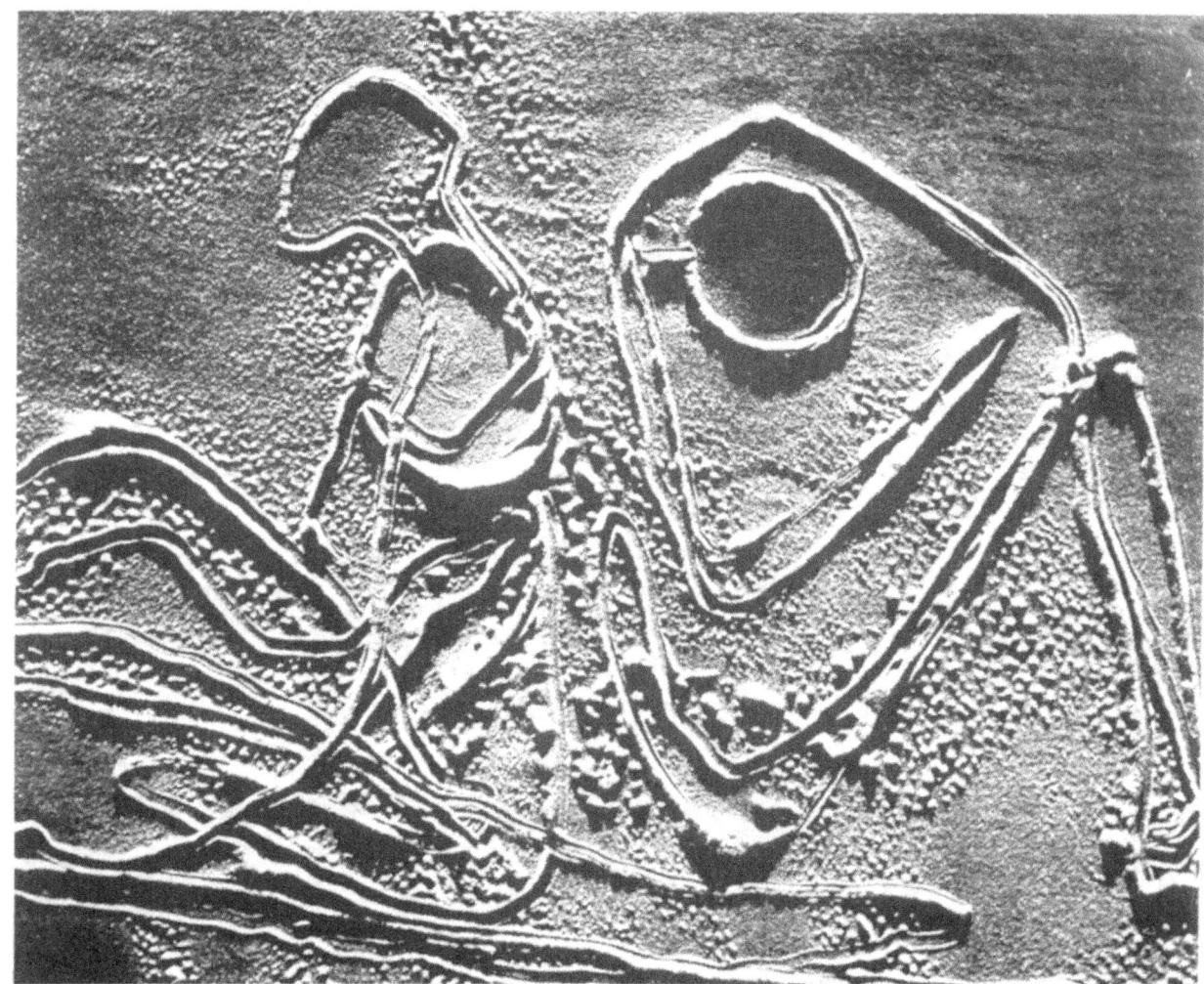

Plate 16 This image was made on a black surface. After tapping the support from underneath to produce the pebble appearance, I poured sand from a paper funnel with a very small opening. The dark head on the right is the result of simply pushing the sand aside with a fingertip until the black paper was exposed. (*Image XXVII: Adam and Eve*)

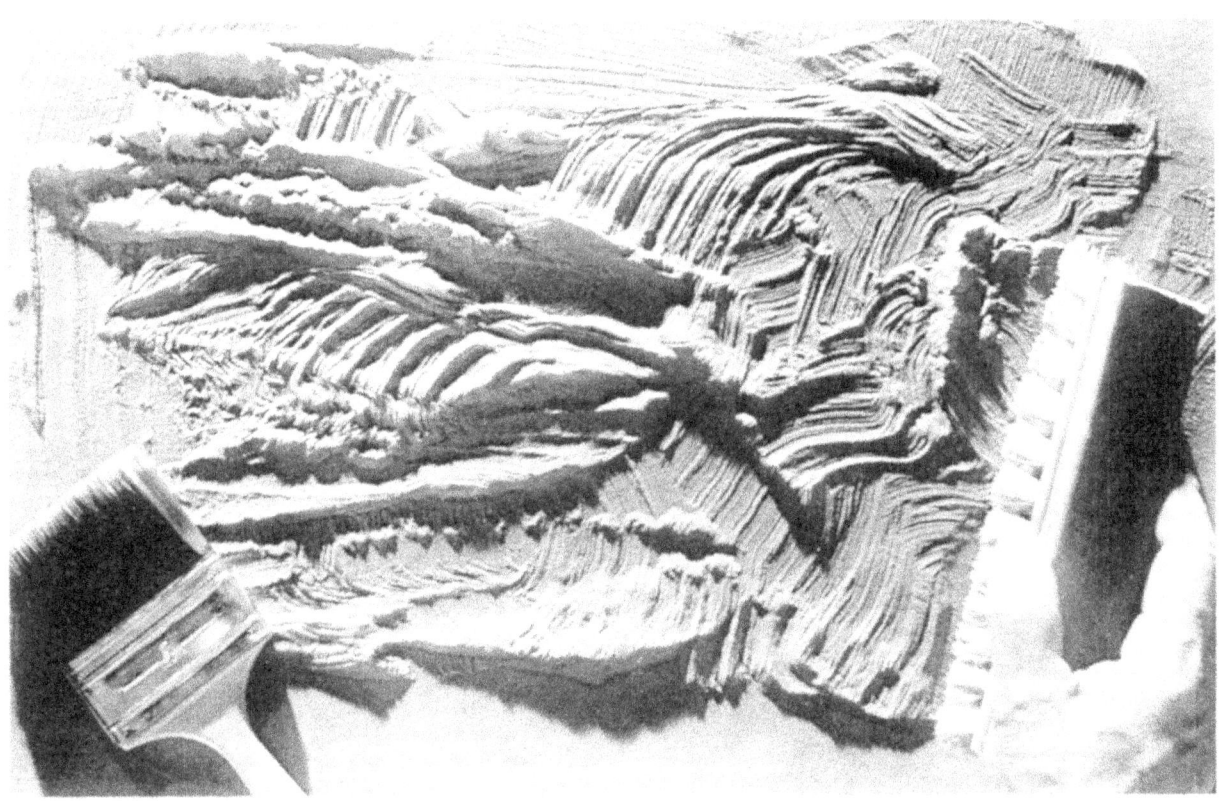

Plate 17 Brushes will create unusual flowing textures.

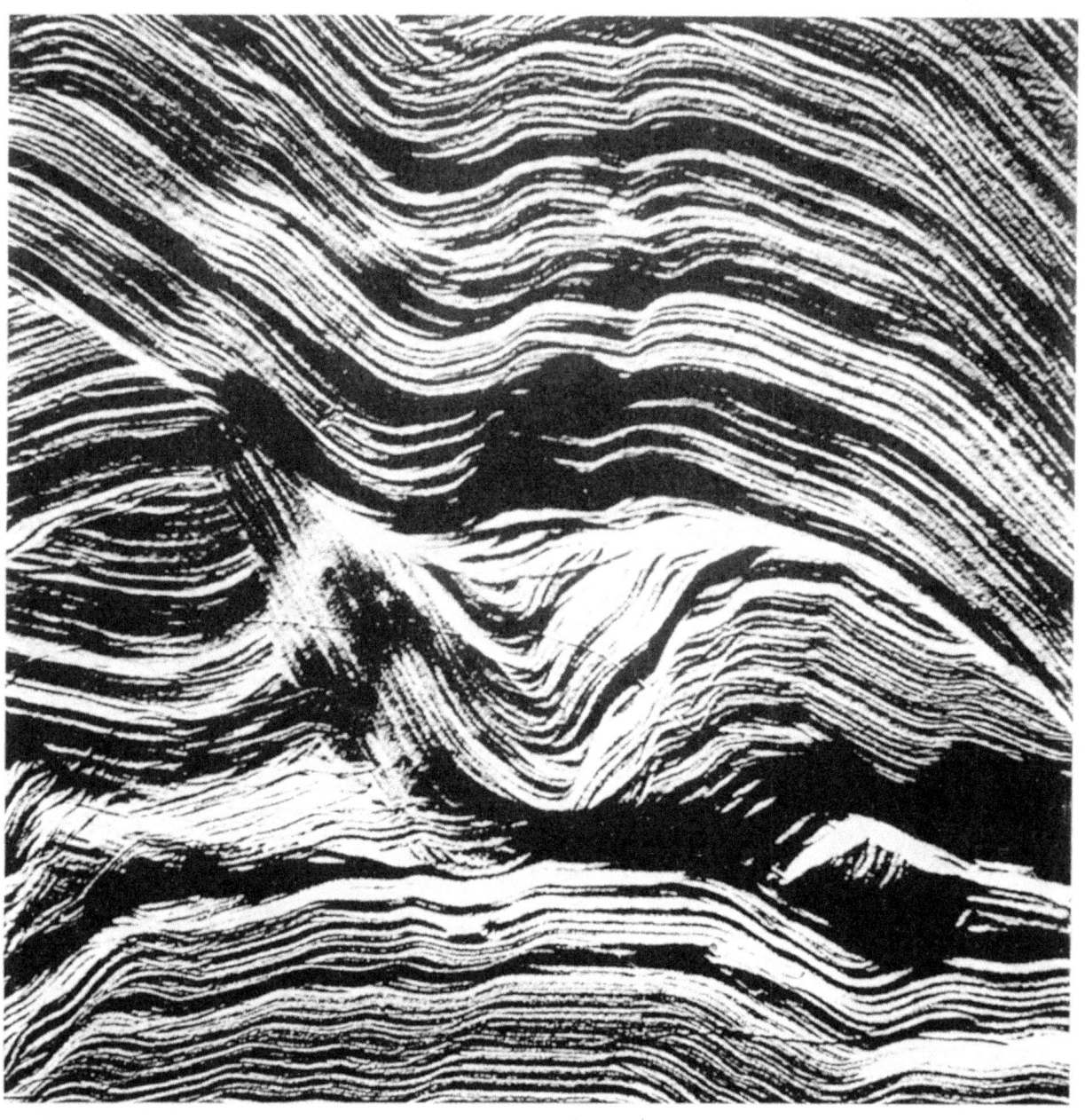

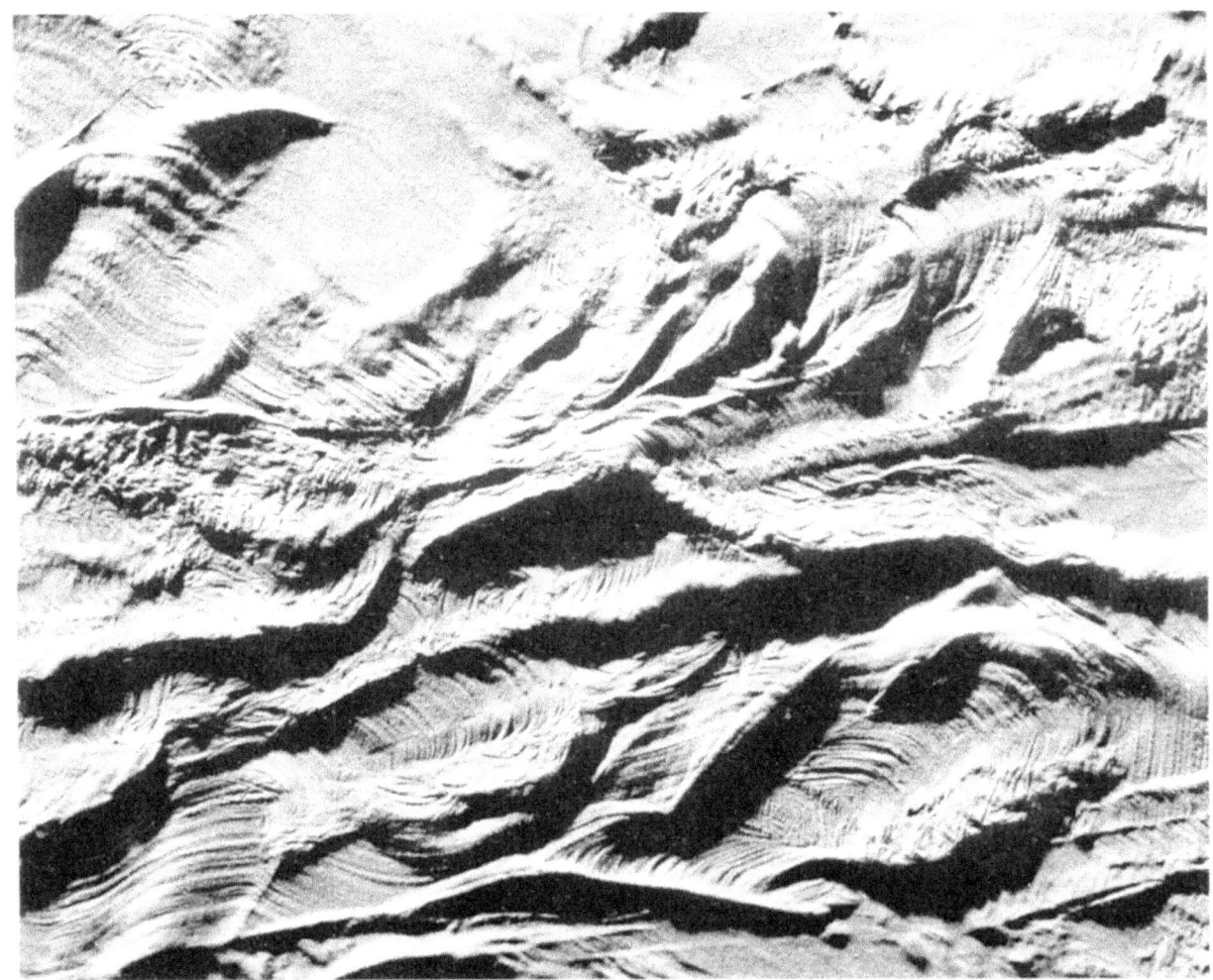

Plate 18 (opposite) **and Plate 19** (above) Different
brushes and different types of strokes produce varied
effects. (*Image XXXIII: Rapids; Image CXVII: Storm*)

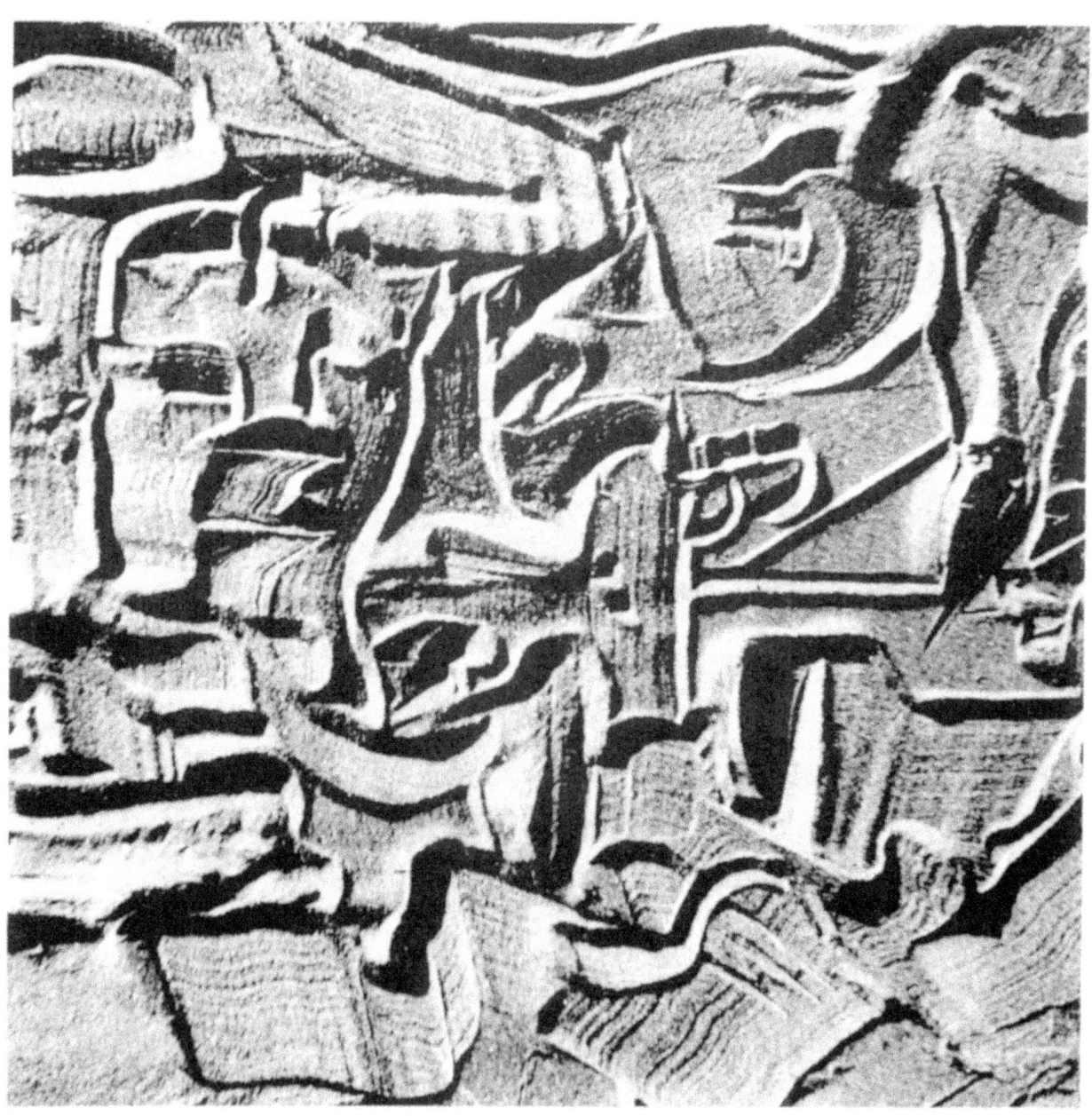

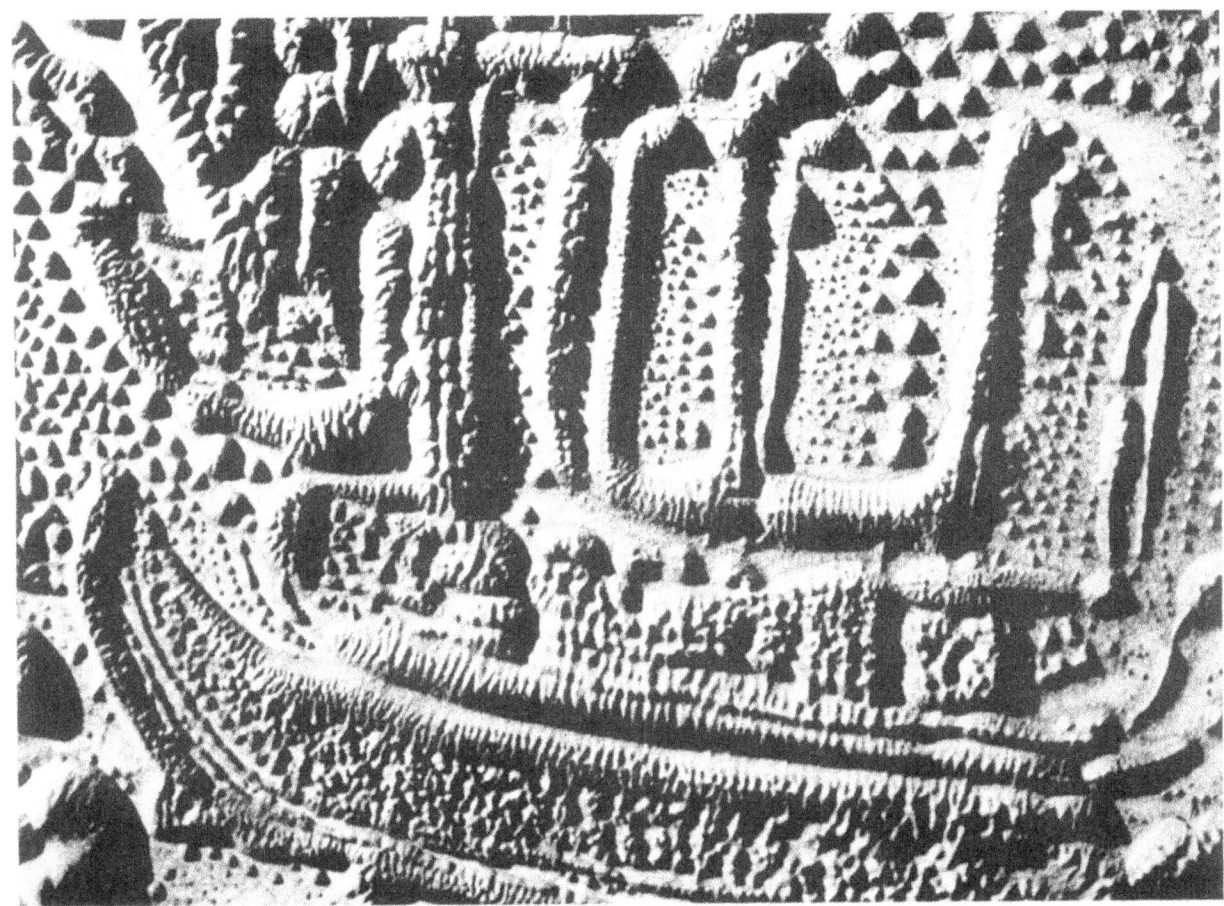

Plate 20 (opposite) The sand was pushed around with a trowel-type palette knife. (*Image XIV: Animation*)

Plate 21 (above) This image was also created with a palette knife, but here I tapped the underside of the base, which gave the image a weather-beaten look. (*Image XVI*)

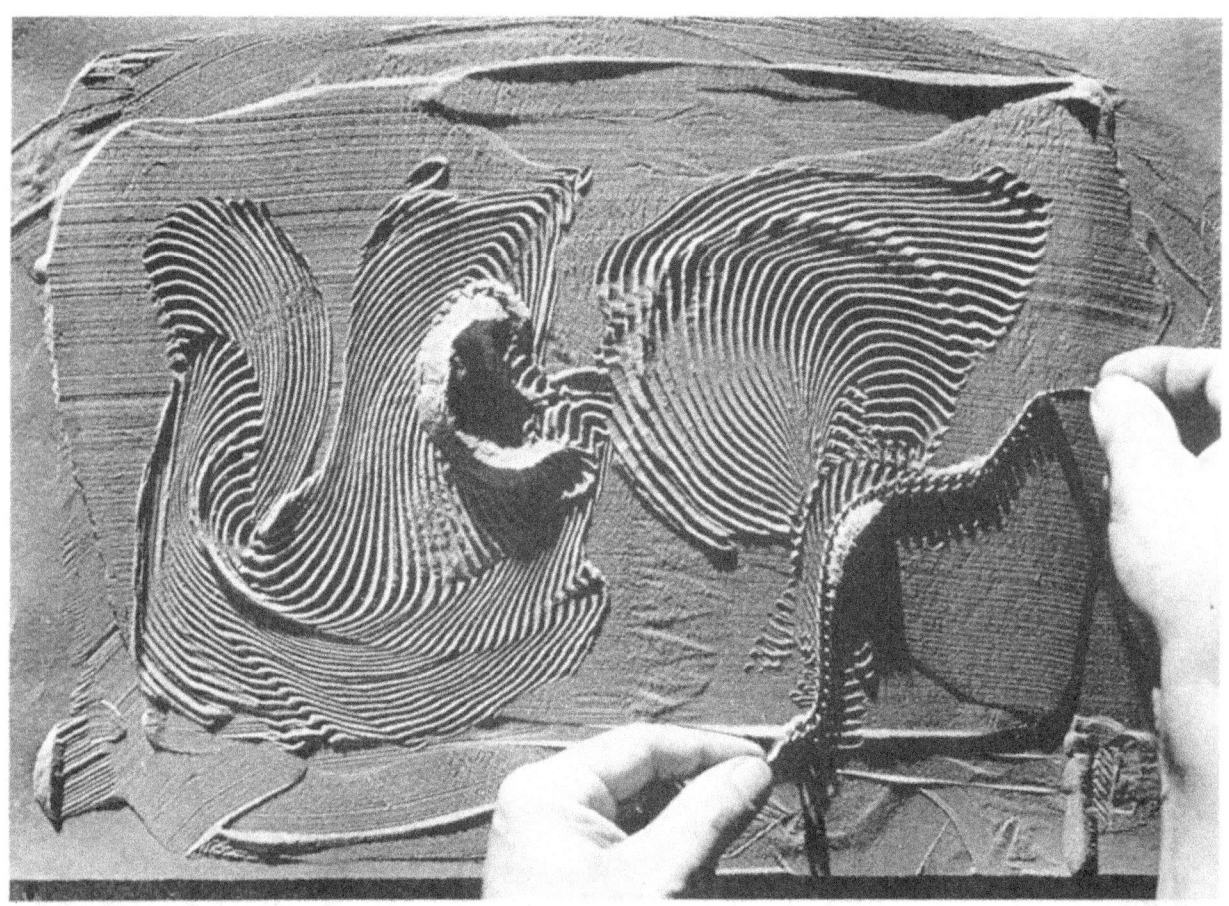

Plate 22 and Plate 23 (opposite) I can think of few media in which chains can be used to create texture. They tend to make whorling, curved patterns in the sand. **(Plate 23: *Image CXXXVII*)**

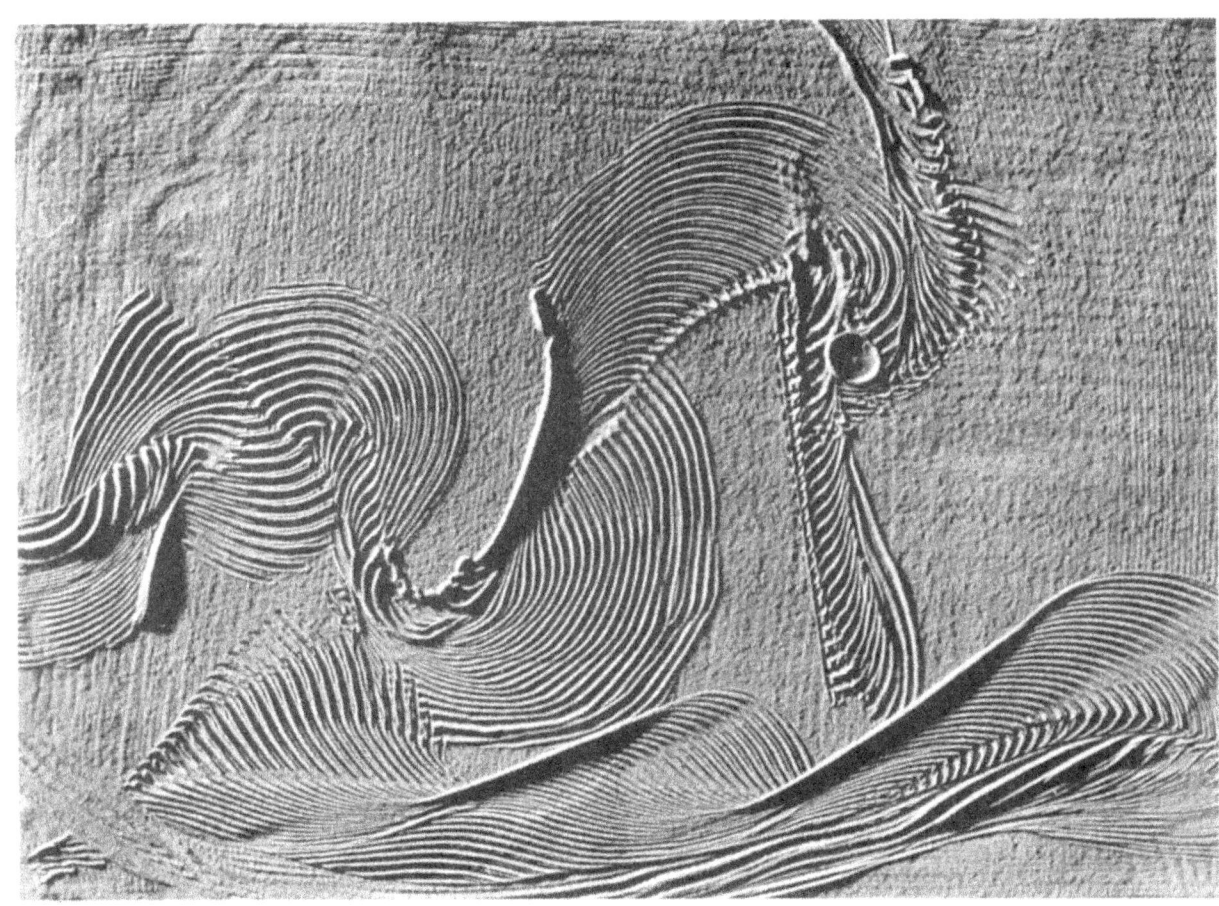

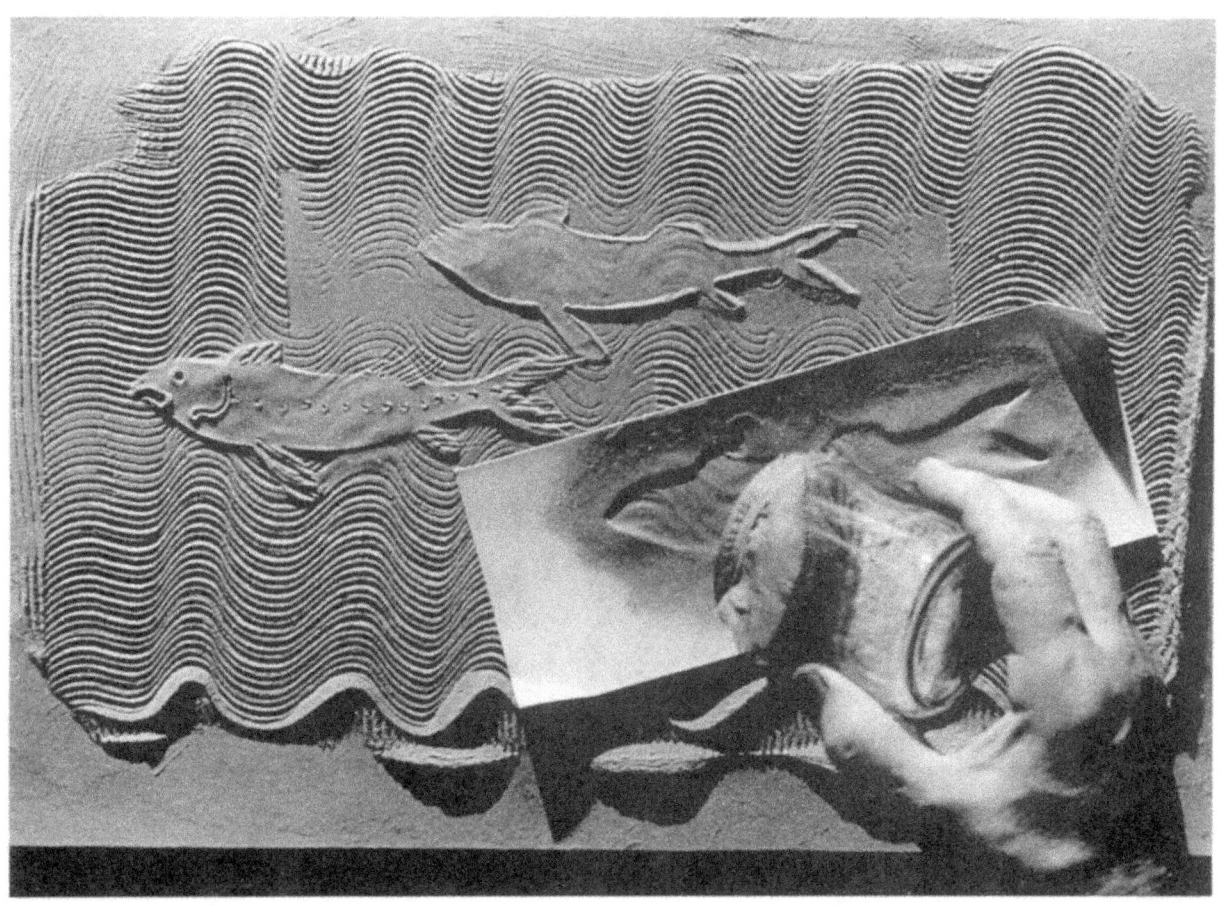

Plate 24 Stencils are useful for making definite images.
The sand may be sifted through silk stretched over a
small jar.

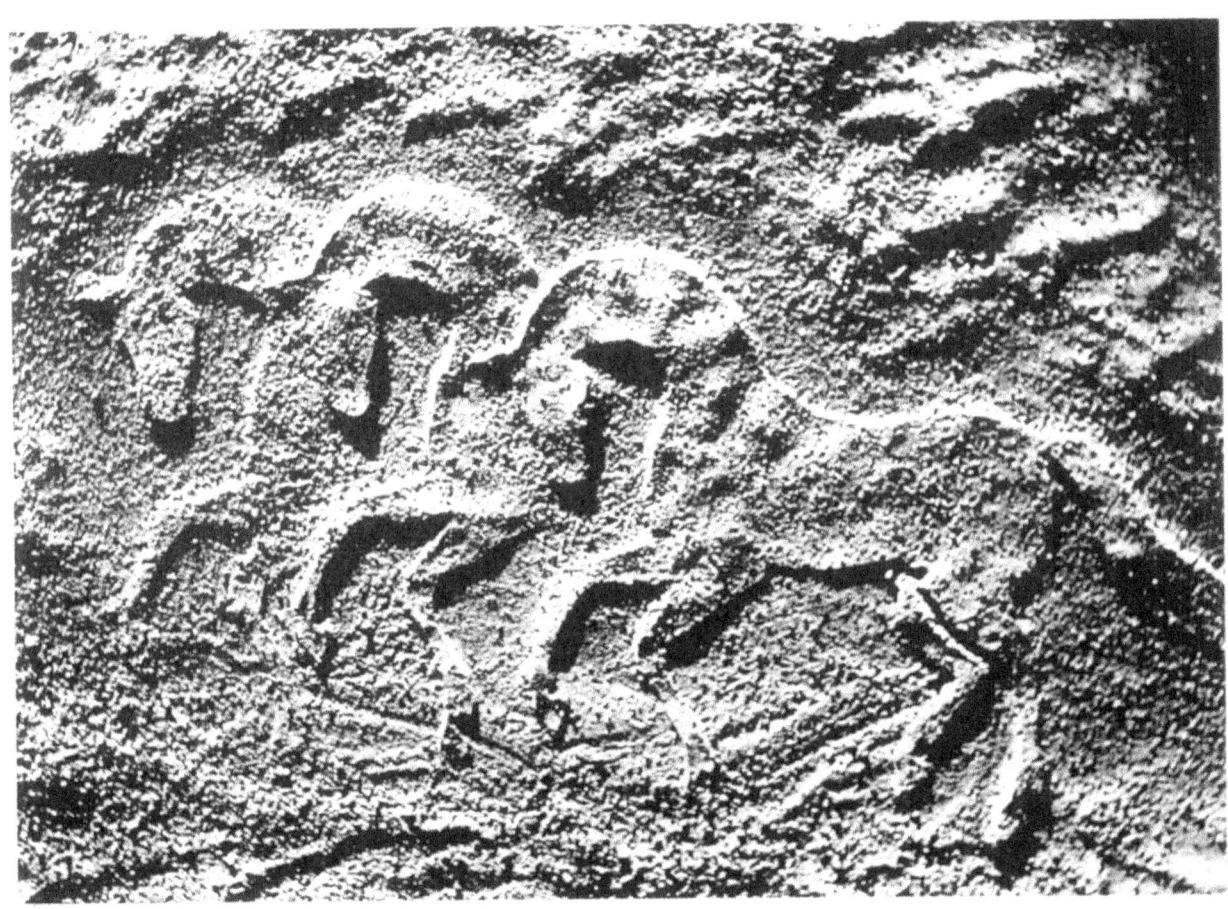

Plate 25 Here I used a stencil cut in an aluminum plate such as is used in offset printing, and as a final step I dropped a coarser sand onto the image from a height.
(*Image XL: Troika*)

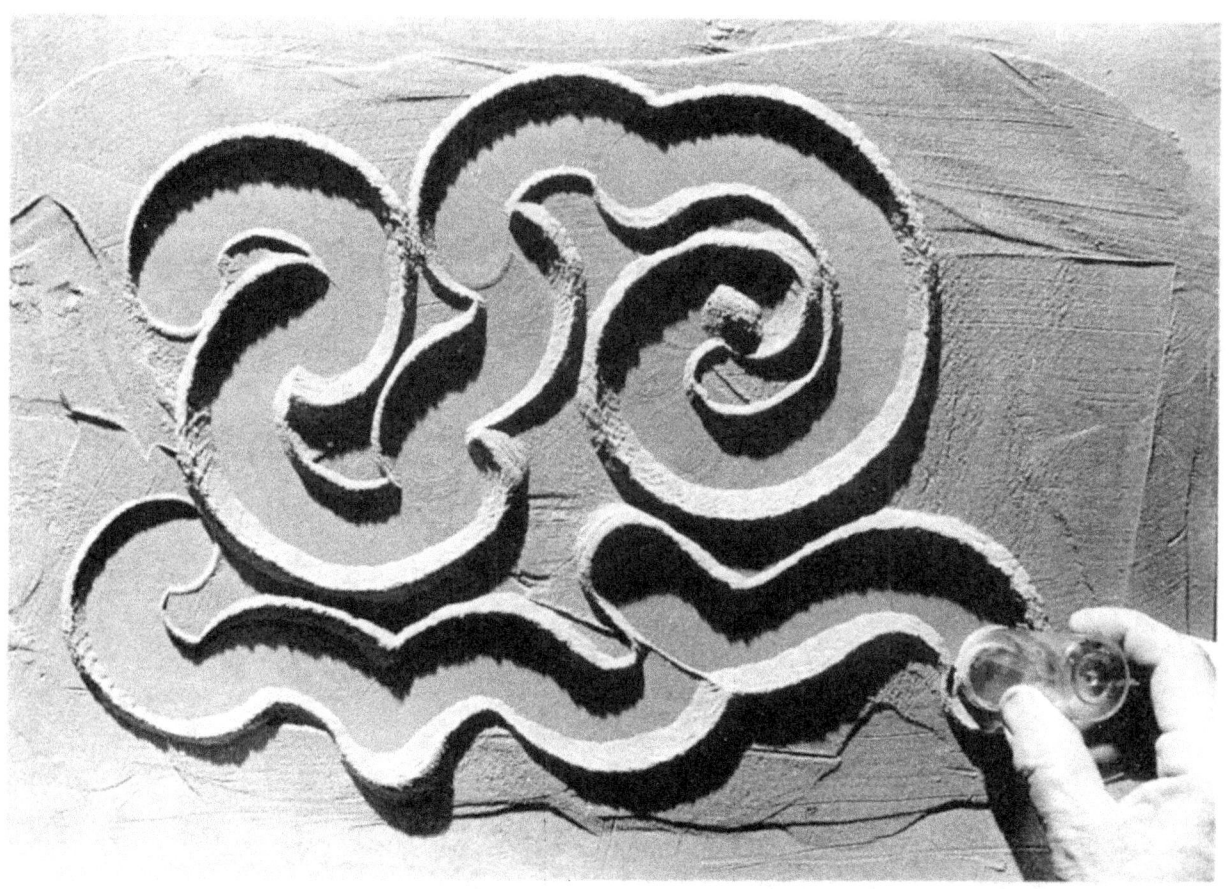

Plate 26 A flat circular tip will create raised parallel lines.

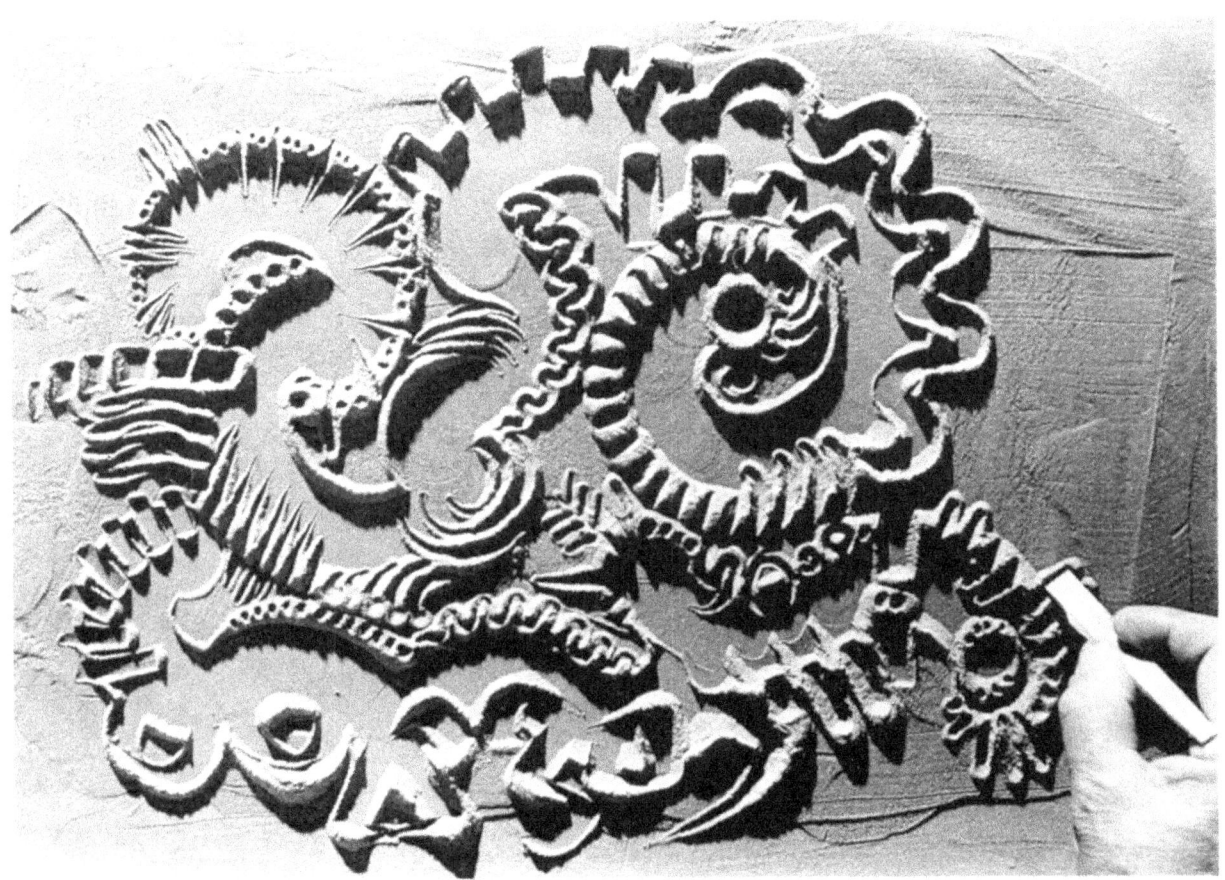

Plate 27 This is the same design as in the preceding plate. Pointed and chisel-shaped tools were used to create the ornamentation.

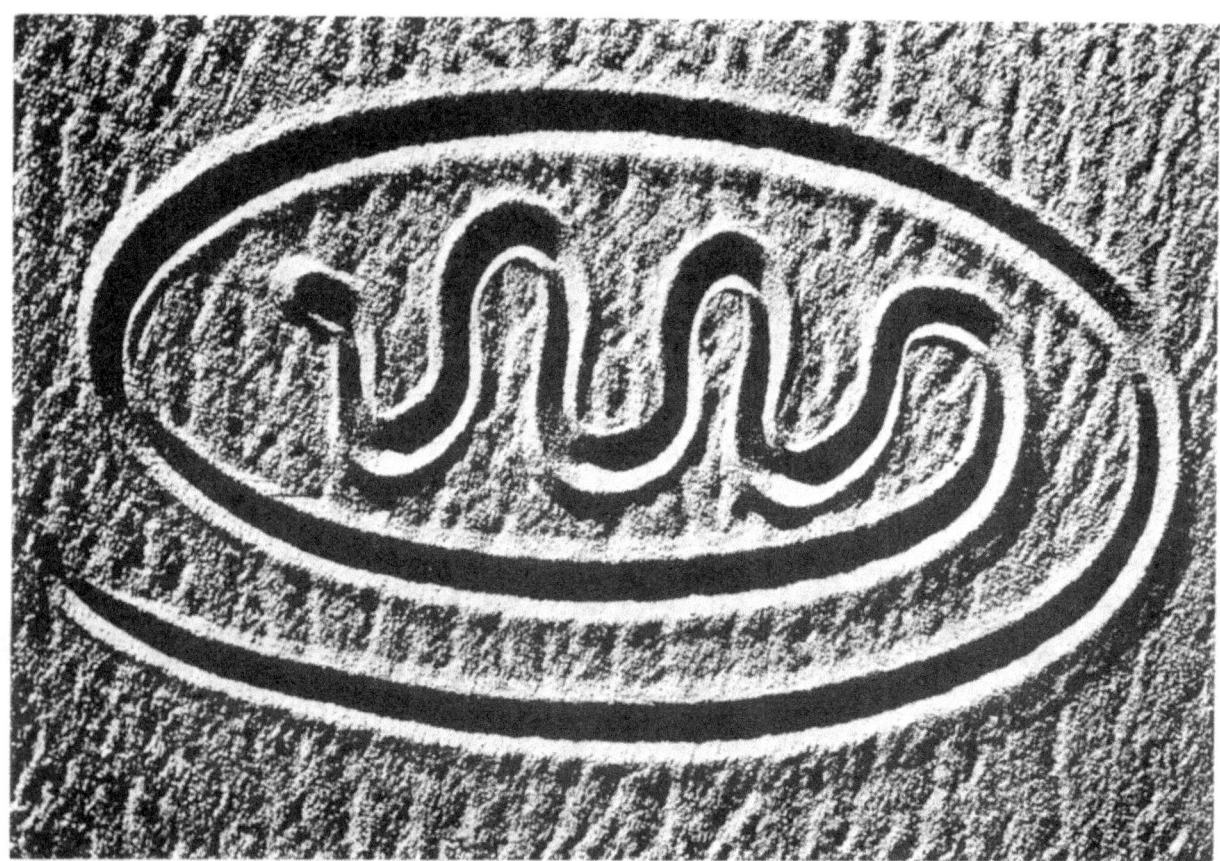

Plate 28 I designed this as my personal hallmark, and I have since used it on my prints and exhibition posters. The background texture was created by moving a straightedge rapidly over the surface of the sand before drawing into it. (*Image I*)

Plate 29 (opposite) The basic design here was formed by moving a jar lid around in the sand. The ornamentation was done with a pointed instrument. (*Image LXXXIII*)

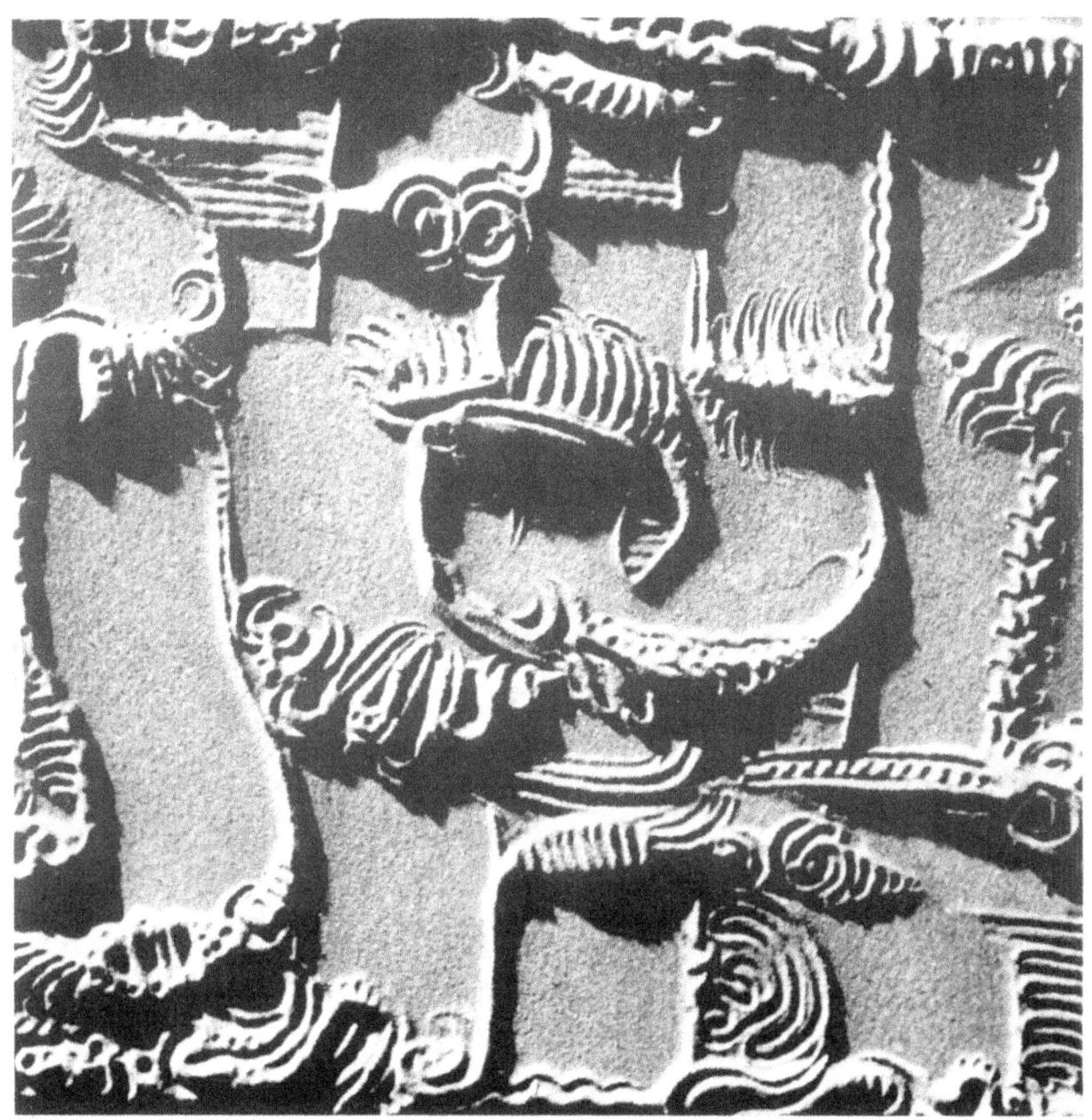

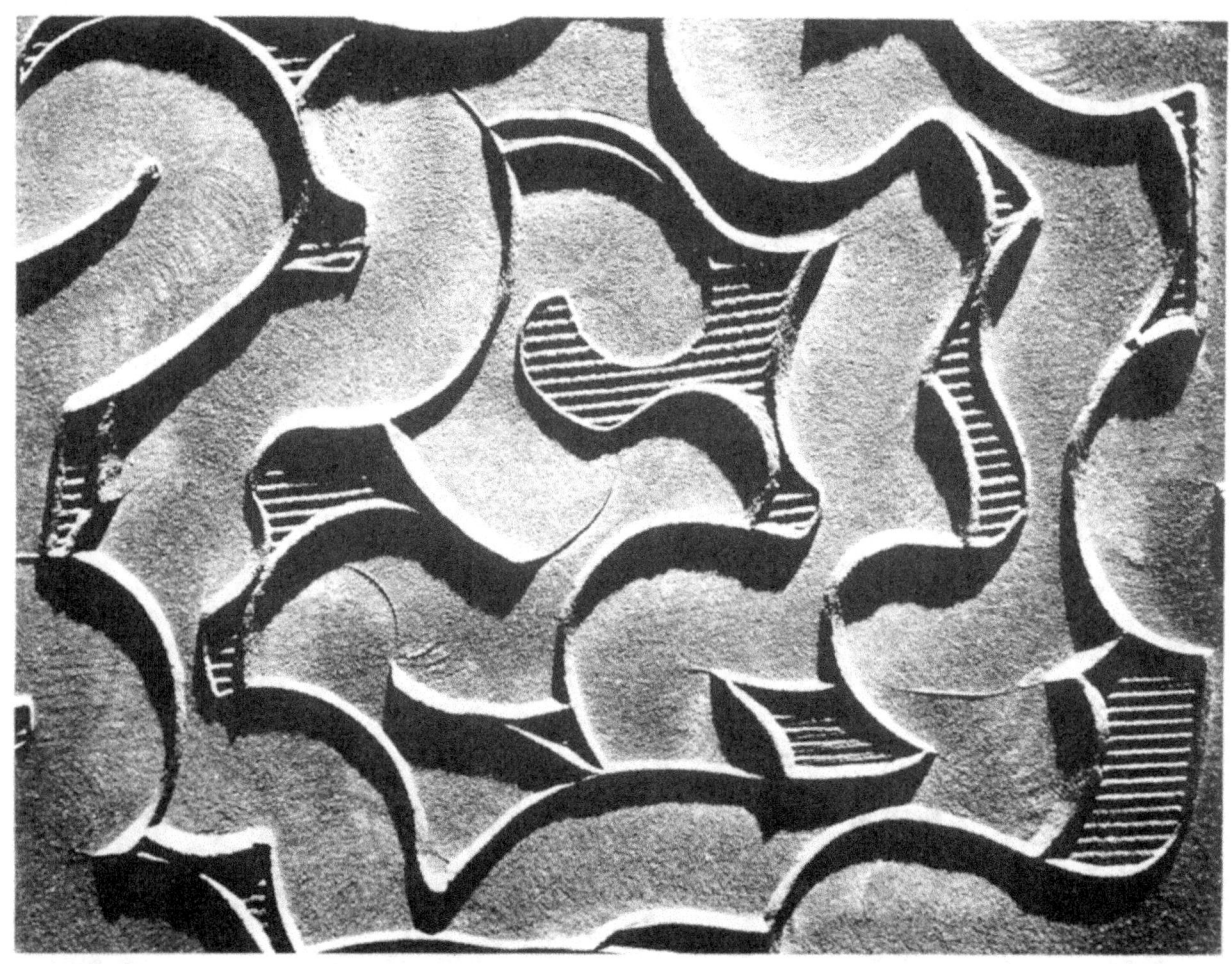

Plate 30 and Plate 31 (opposite) Again, one can obtain
a great variety of effects by combining techniques. Here
I smoothed the sand to a thickness of somewhat less
than an eighth of an inch, used a comb to give the sand
a basic texture, and then moved a jar lid
around in the sand to give the image its final appearance.
(*Image XXVI; Image LXX*)

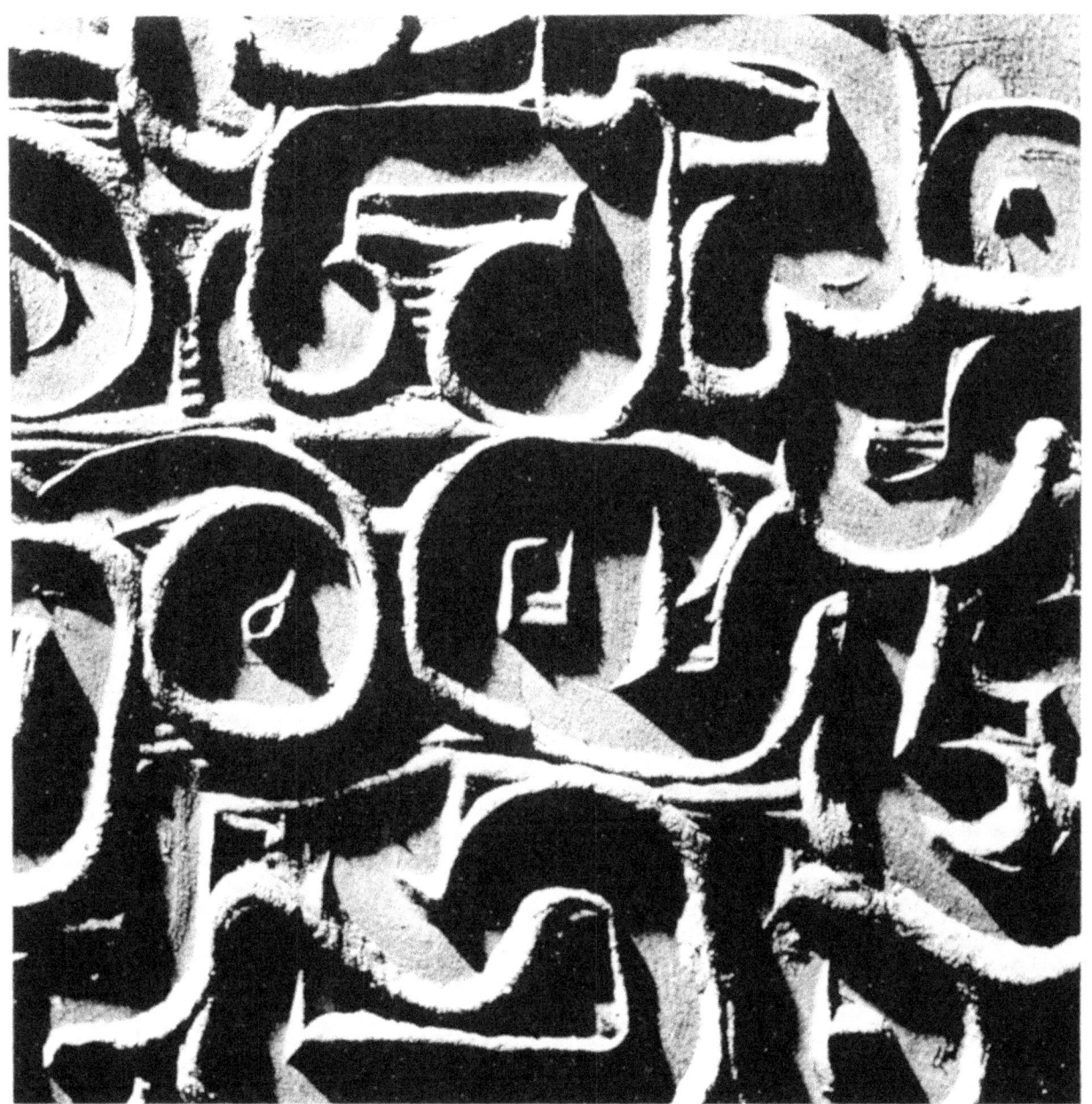

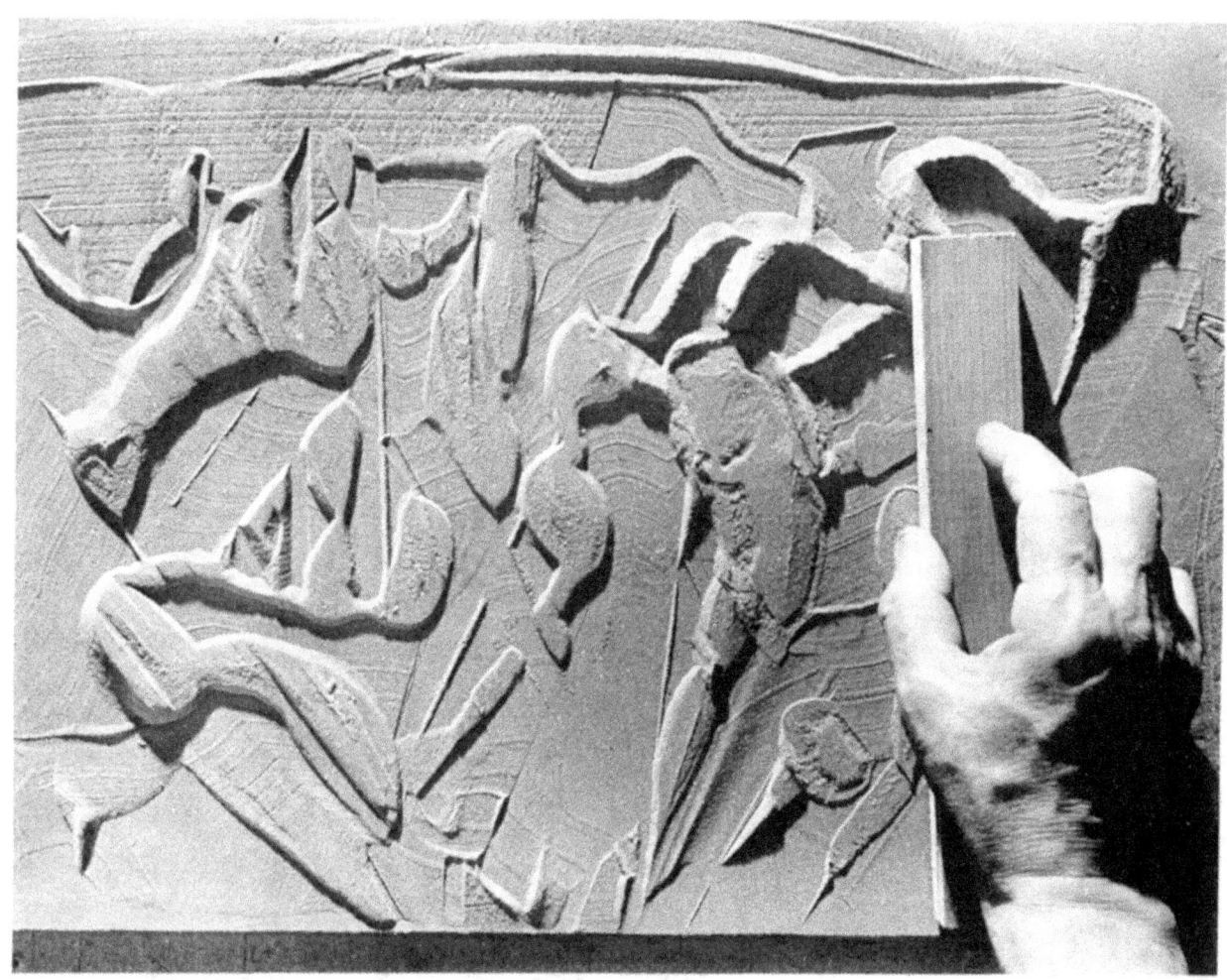

Plate 32 A variety of raised shapes can be produced by pushing, pulling, and pressing down the sand with a small board.

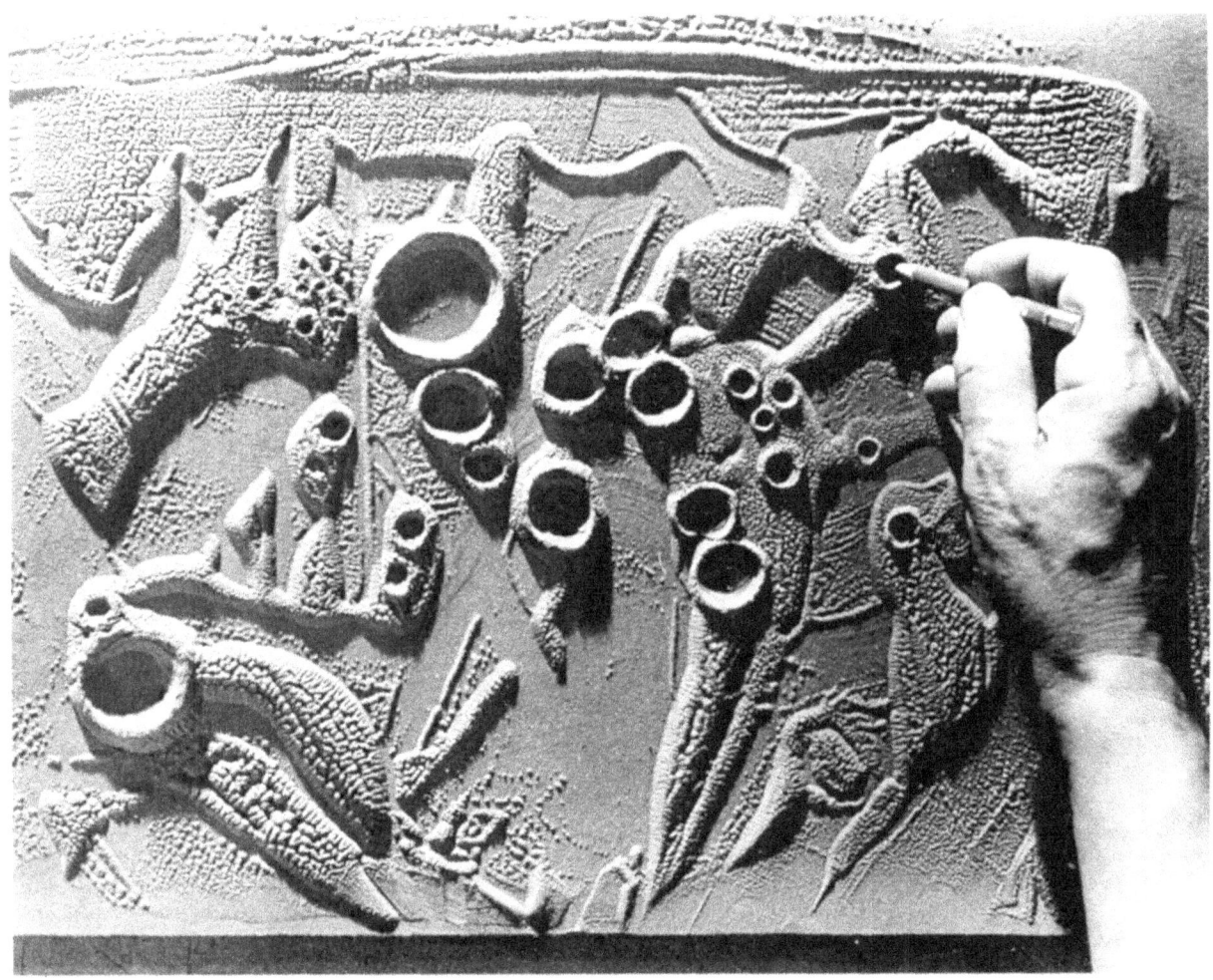

Plate 33 This is the same design as in the preceding plate.
A gentle tapping with a fingertip from underneath the
base will make the sand "pearl." The "craters" are
produced either with the fingertips or with pointed tools.

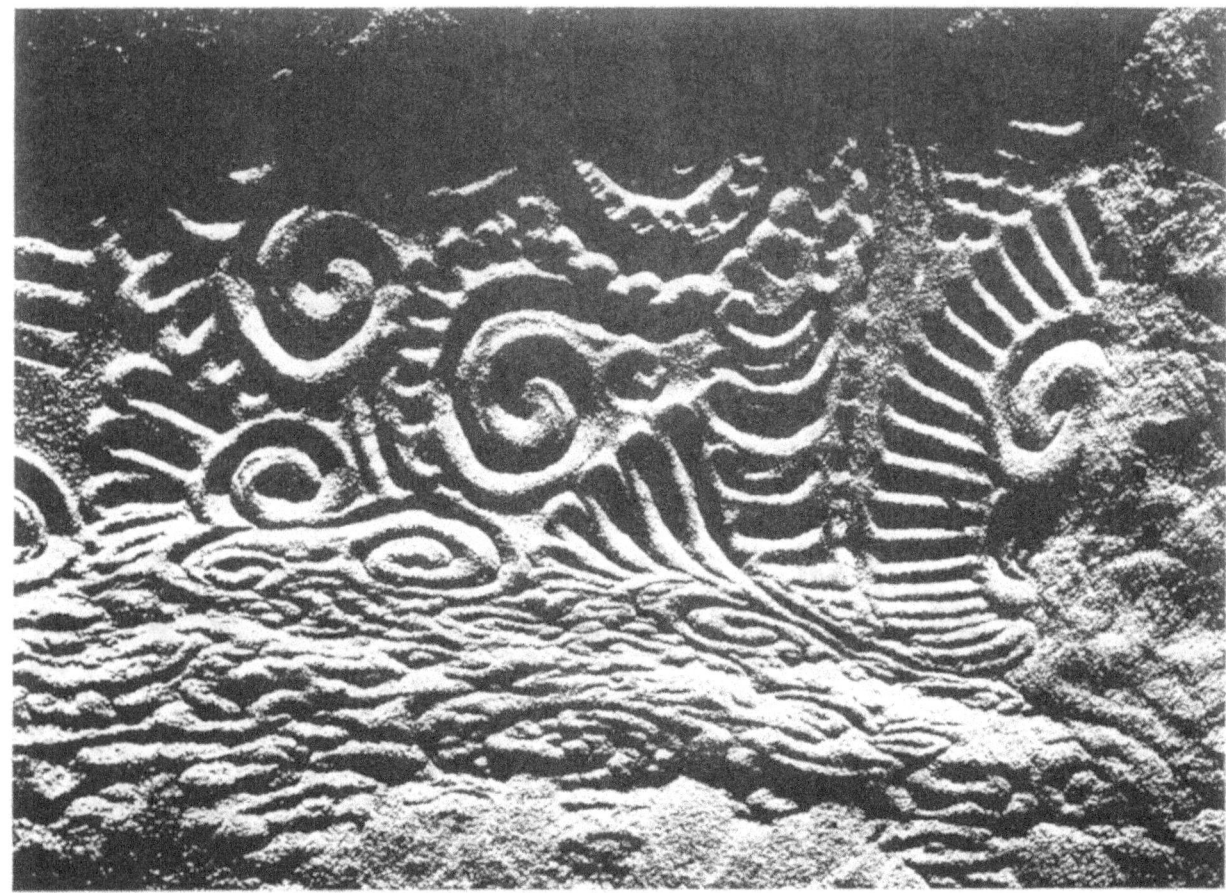

Plate 34 By lifting one edge of the cardboard and letting the sand slide, one can sometimes obtain more compressed images. This example was a lucky accident. Later experiments with the technique have not usually been very successful. (*Image VII: Happening*)

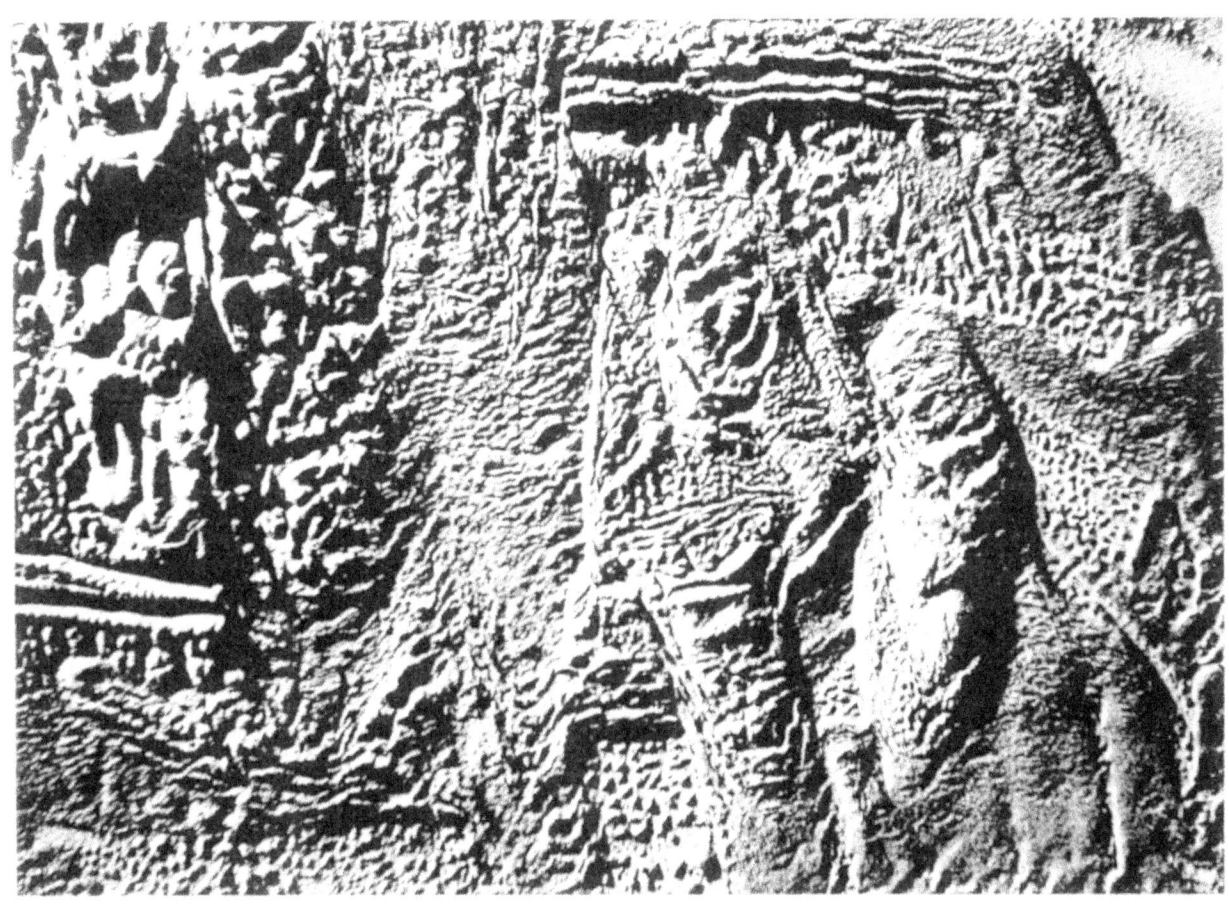

Plate 35 Here the support was lifted just enough to cause the sand to slide a little and then tapped lightly so that the surface appears eroded. (*Image XXXVI: Mrs. Lot*)

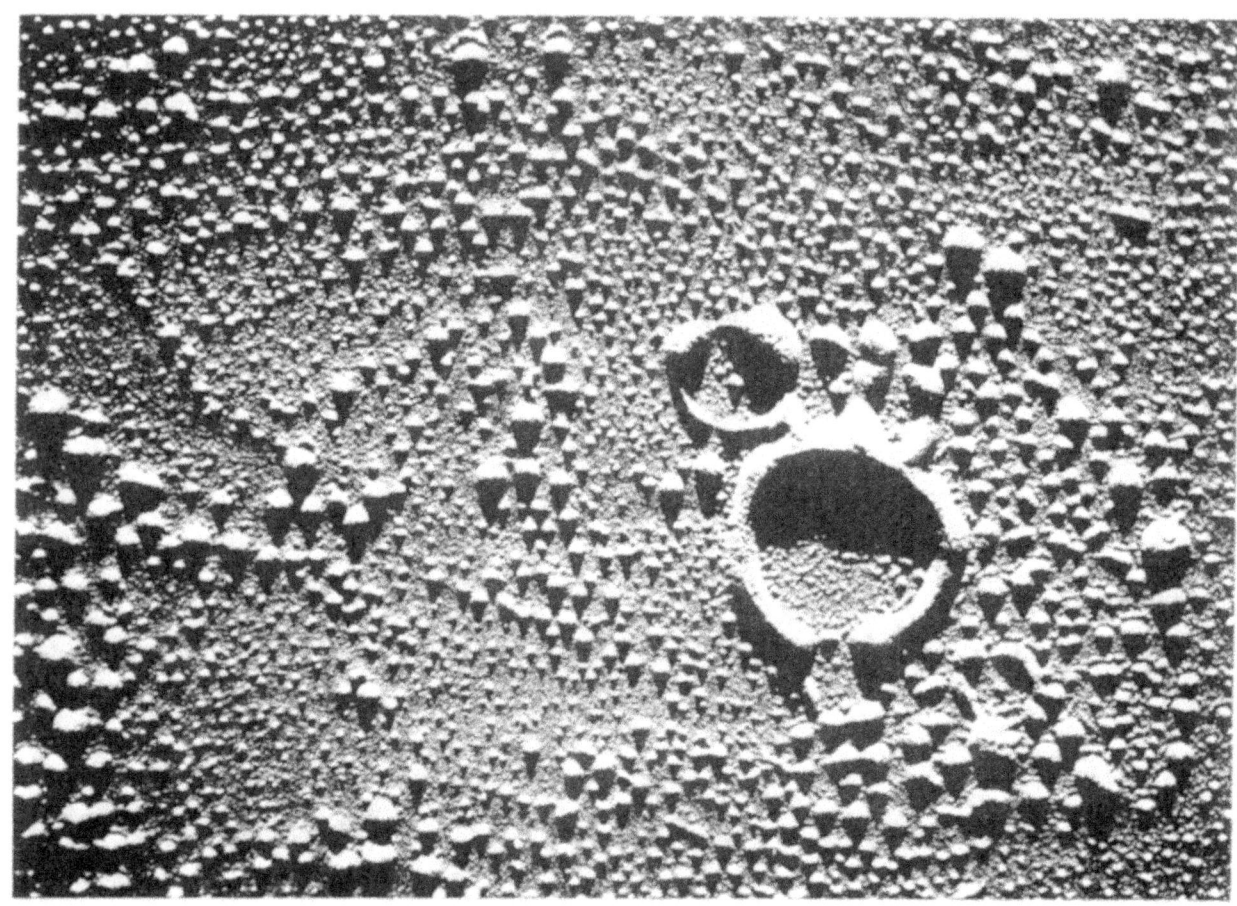

Plate 36 Various other effects can be created by
somehow distorting the image after it has been made.
This image was formed by vibrating the tabletop both before
and after forming the craters. (*Image XIX*)

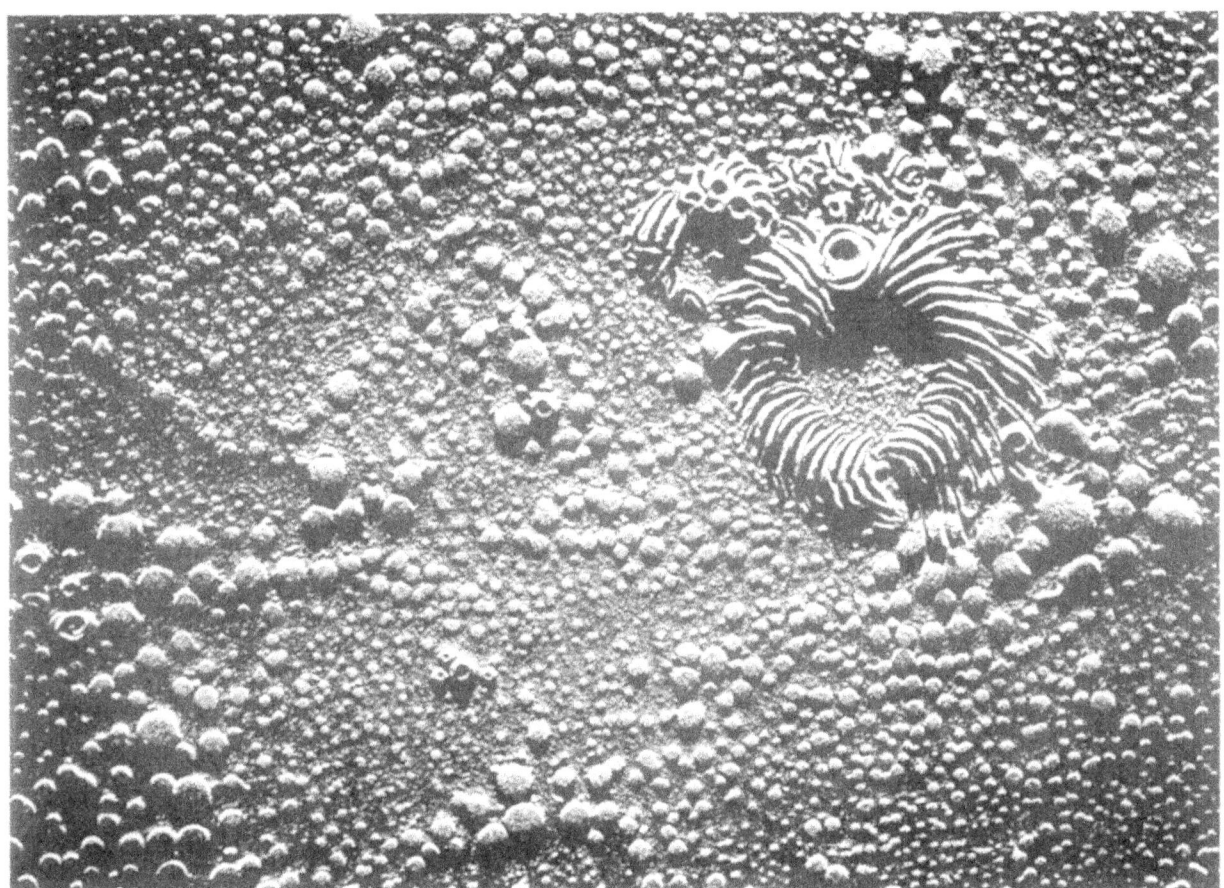

Plate 37 This is the same design as in the preceding
plate. A piece of paper was placed on top of the sand
to flatten the high places and the craters were carved
into with a pointed instrument. (*Image XX: Shallow*)

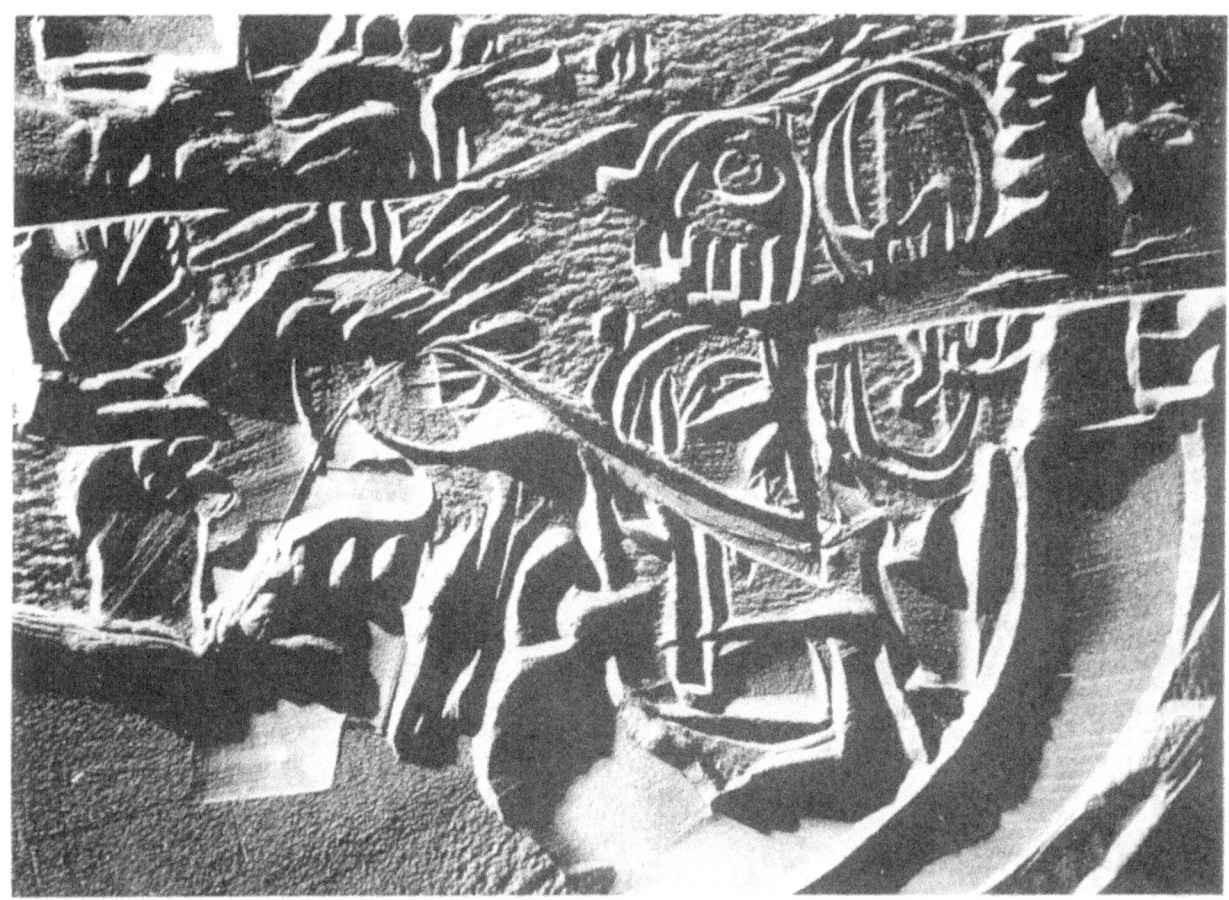

Plate 38 This design was formed on a sheet of paper that had been cut into three curving segments. When the basic design was complete, the pieces of paper were gently pulled a slight distance apart to create this unusual effect. (*Image XXIII*)

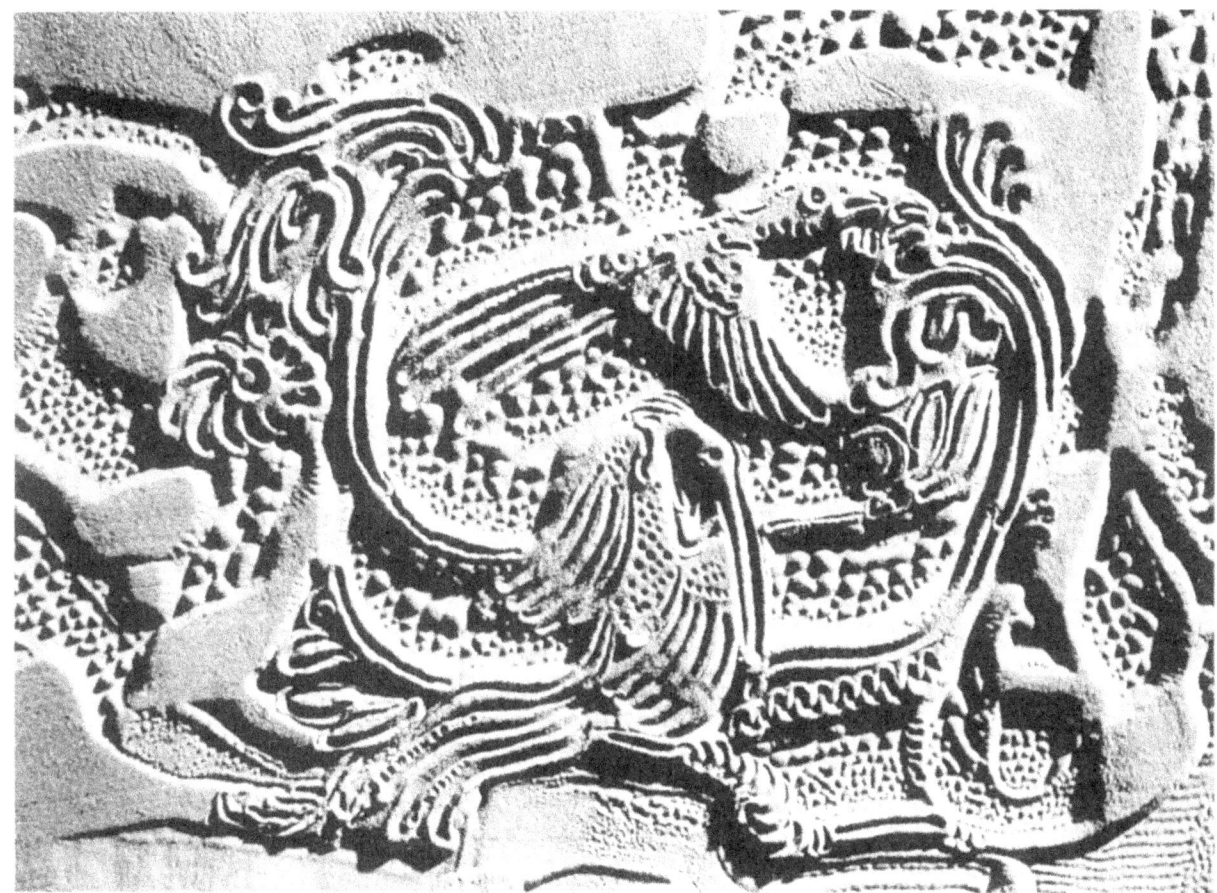

Plate 39 For this image I drew into the sand with a pointed instrument while the table underneath was being vibrated. I then flattened the top levels with a piece of paper and added a few more strokes to complete the composition. (*Image XXIX: Bird Relief*)

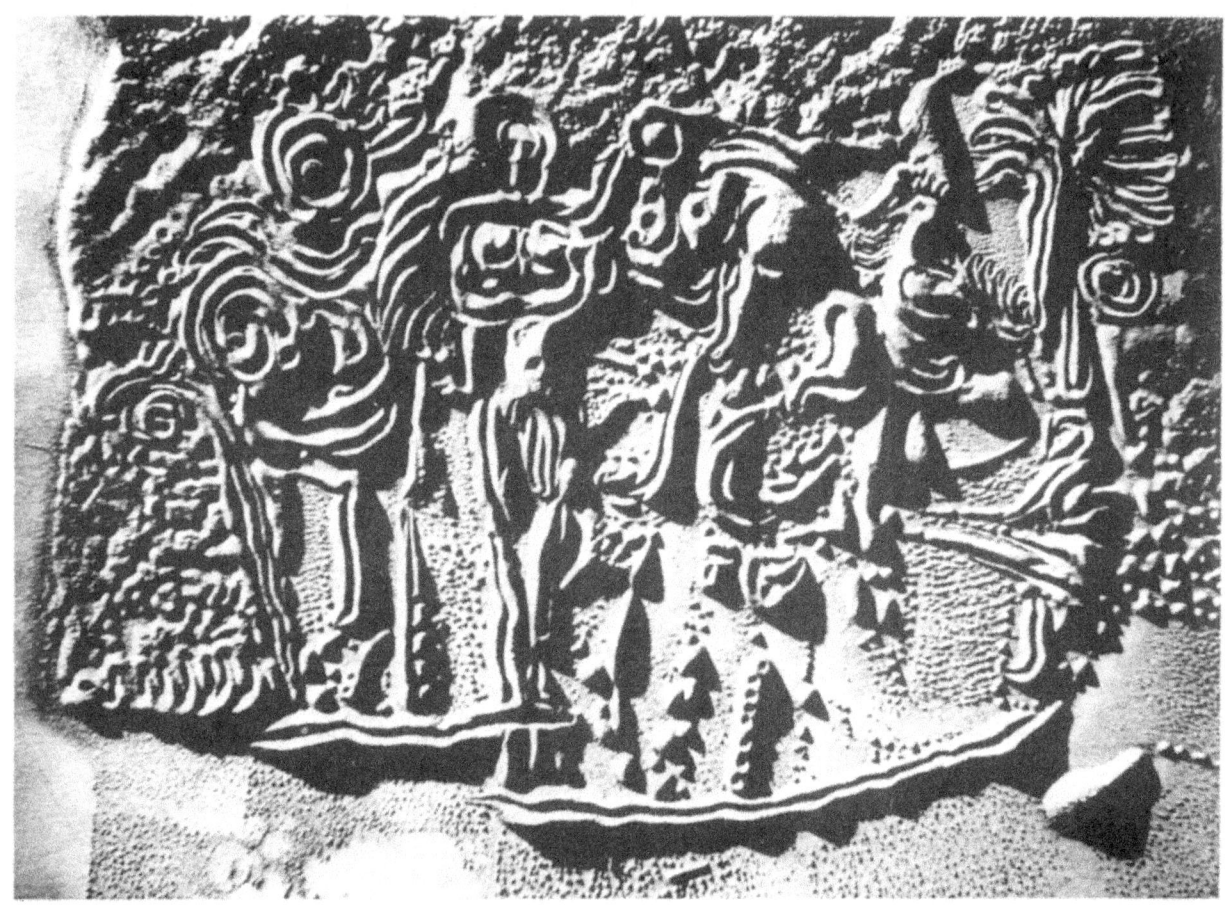

Plate 40 The figures in this image emerged by accident
as I was developing the composition, and I decided to
make them central to the image. (*Image XXX*)

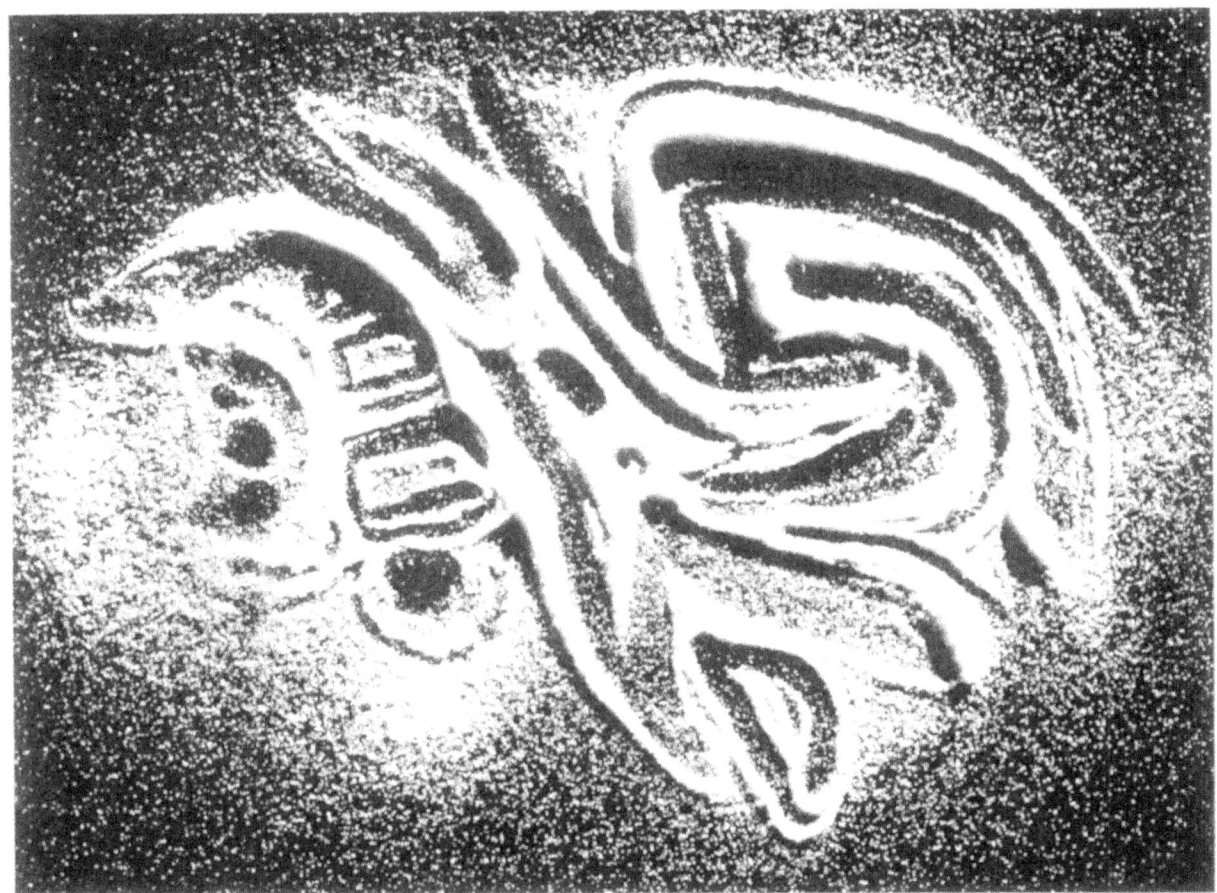

Plate 41 This image was made with table salt on black
paper. Sand of finer grit is considerably more versatile
than salt, especially when fine details are desired, but
salt and other gritty substances offer a variety of
possibilities for design. (*Image XXXIX*)

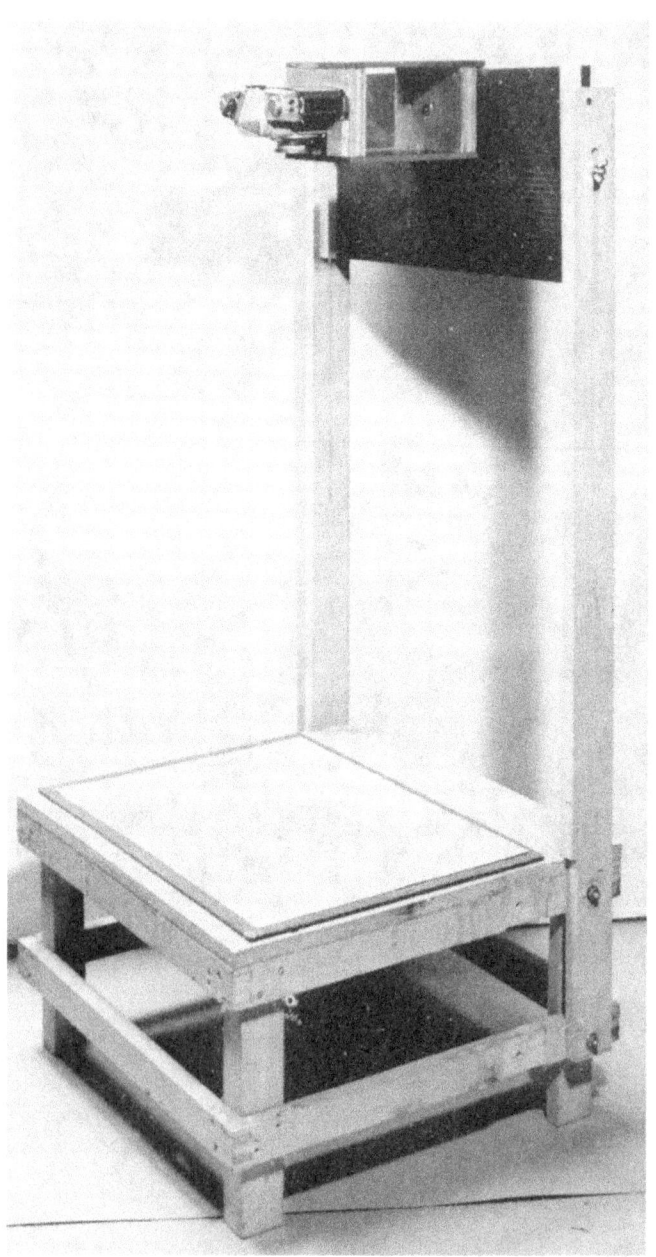

Plate 42 I built this easel specifically for photographing my sand images. The camera can be raised and lowered so as to include larger or smaller portions of the total Masonite surface in the photograph, depending on how much area the image itself covers. A light about fifteen feet away, placed very low, makes for a good play of light and shadow. The easel can be turned to get the best angle of light for the particular image. I use a 35mm camera, and I get best results with Kodak Panatomix X or High Contrast Copy film.

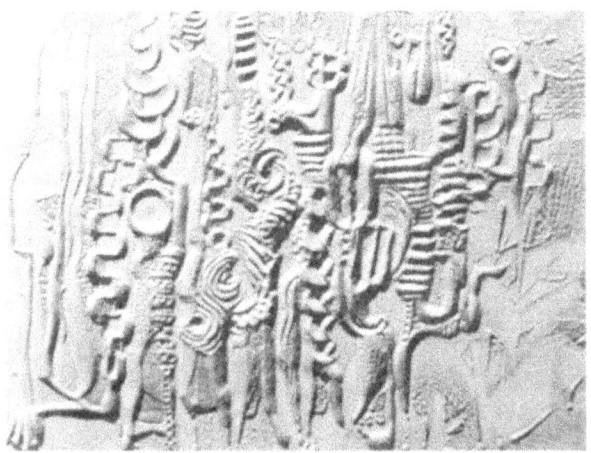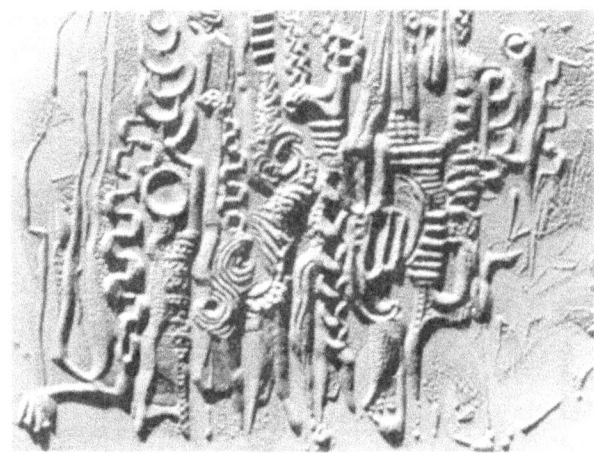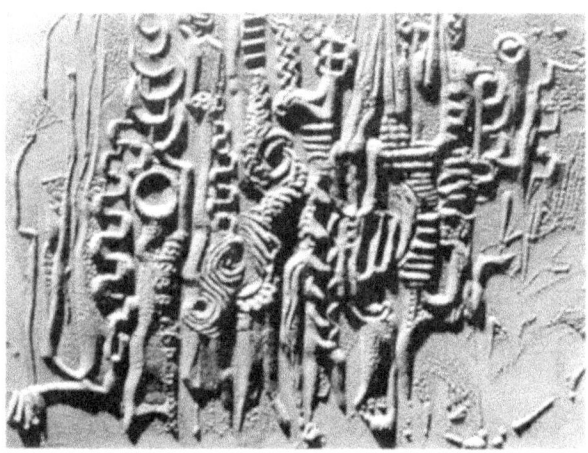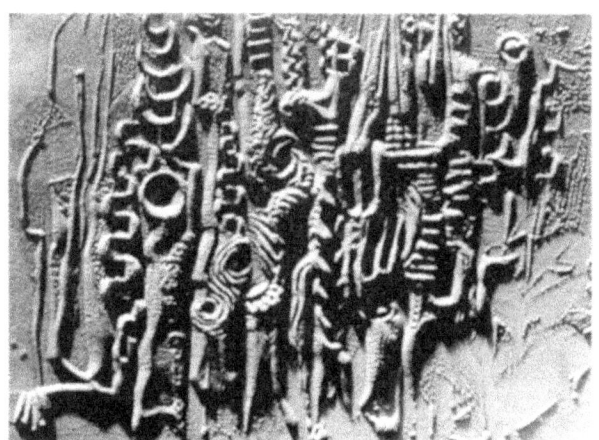

Plates 43—46 One should experiment to find the best lighting before photographing. This series shows how the play of light and shadow changes when the source of light is lowered.

Images

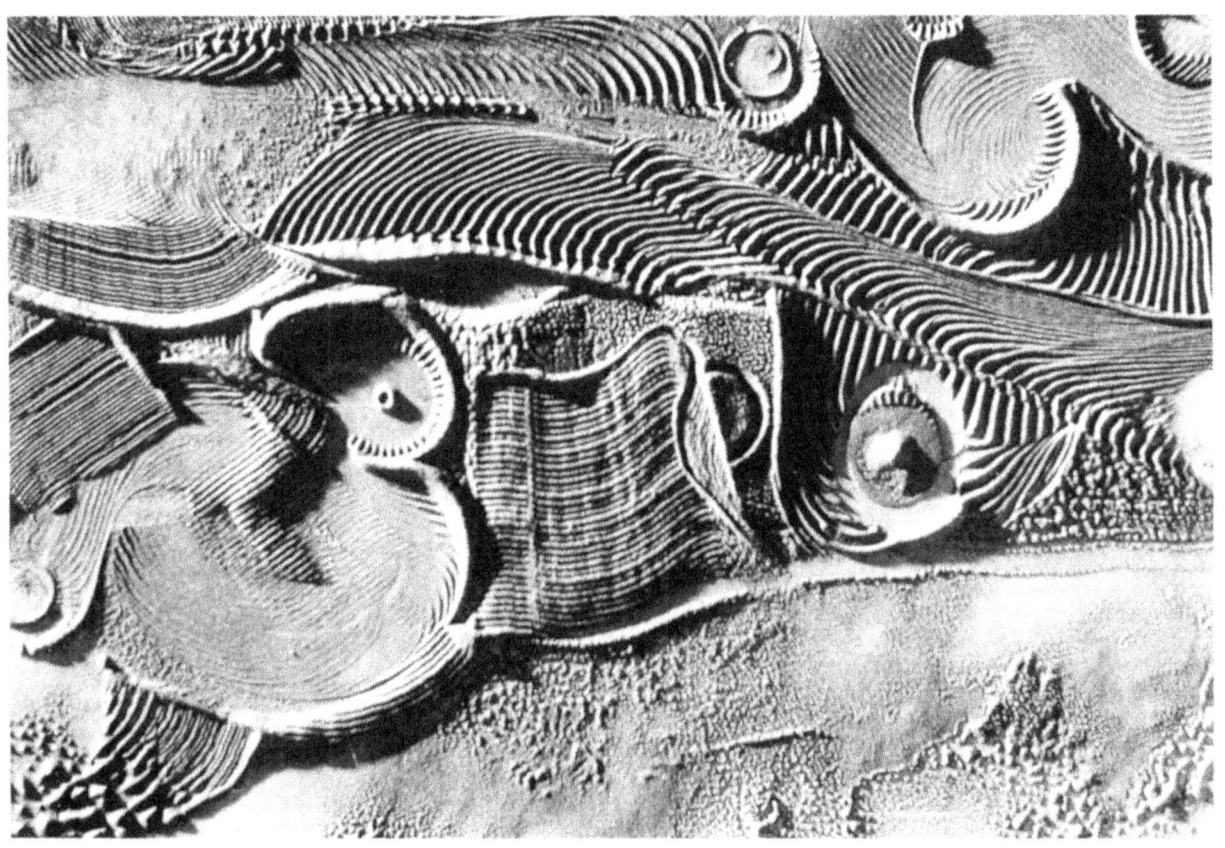

CLXXV

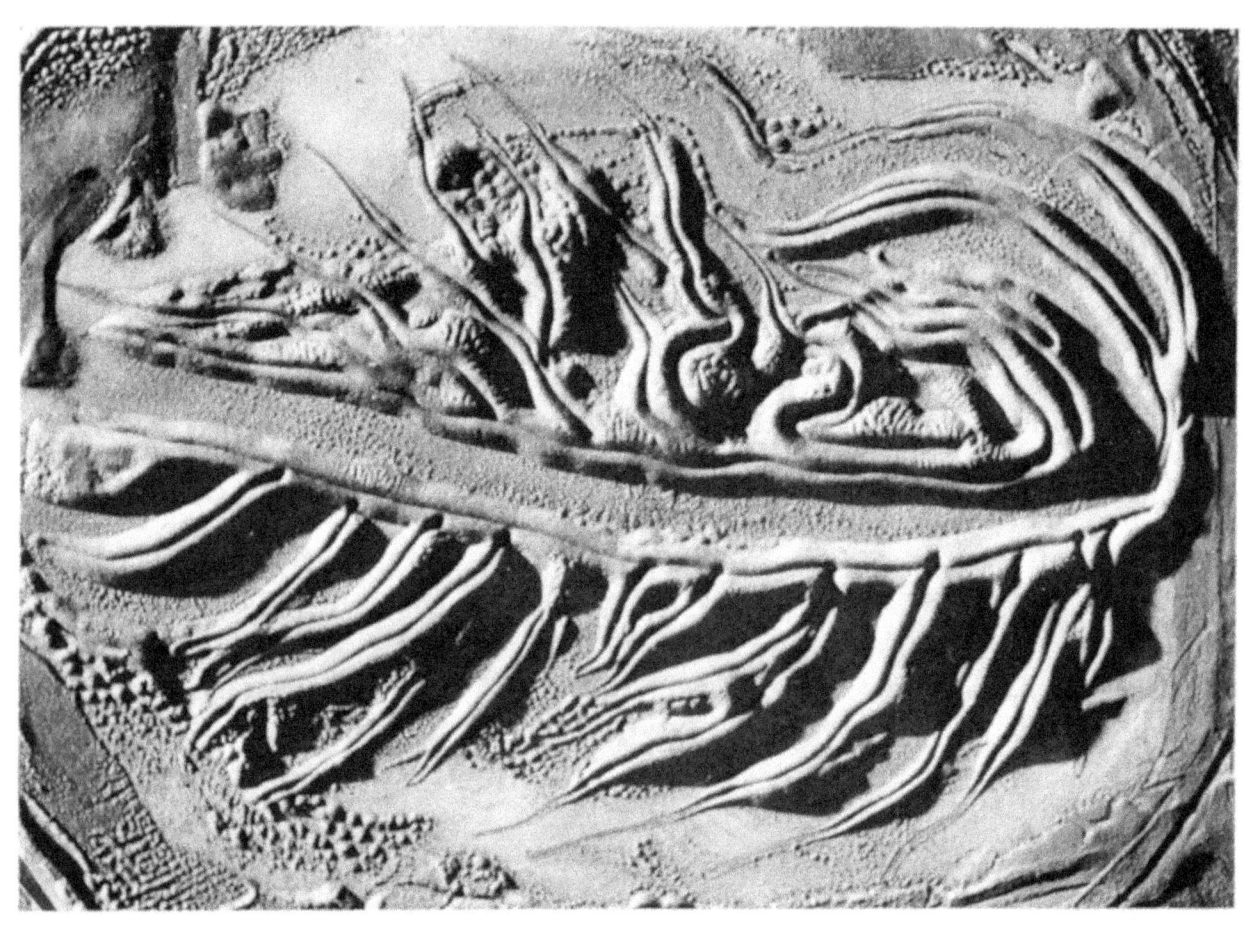

LVI Petrified Leaf

CLXII (opposite)

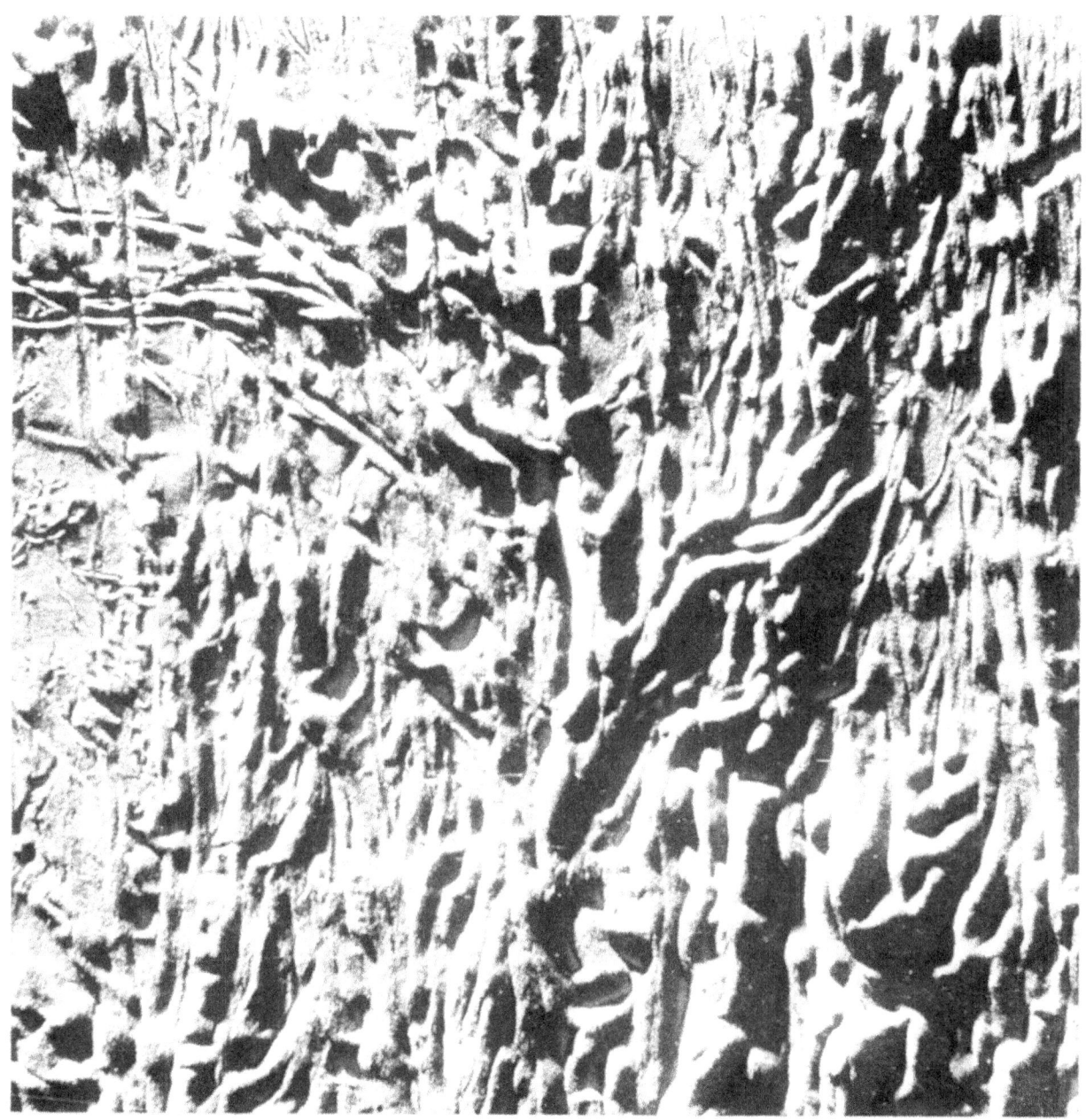

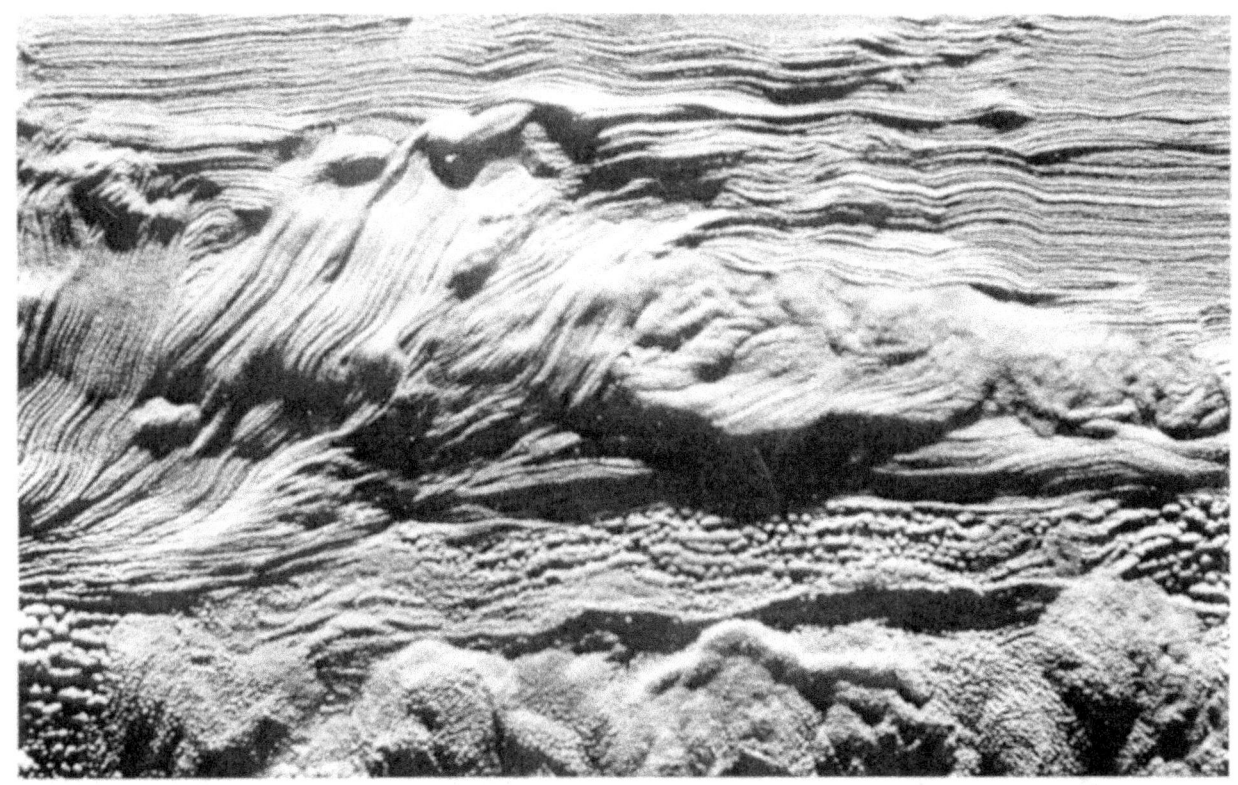

CLXVI

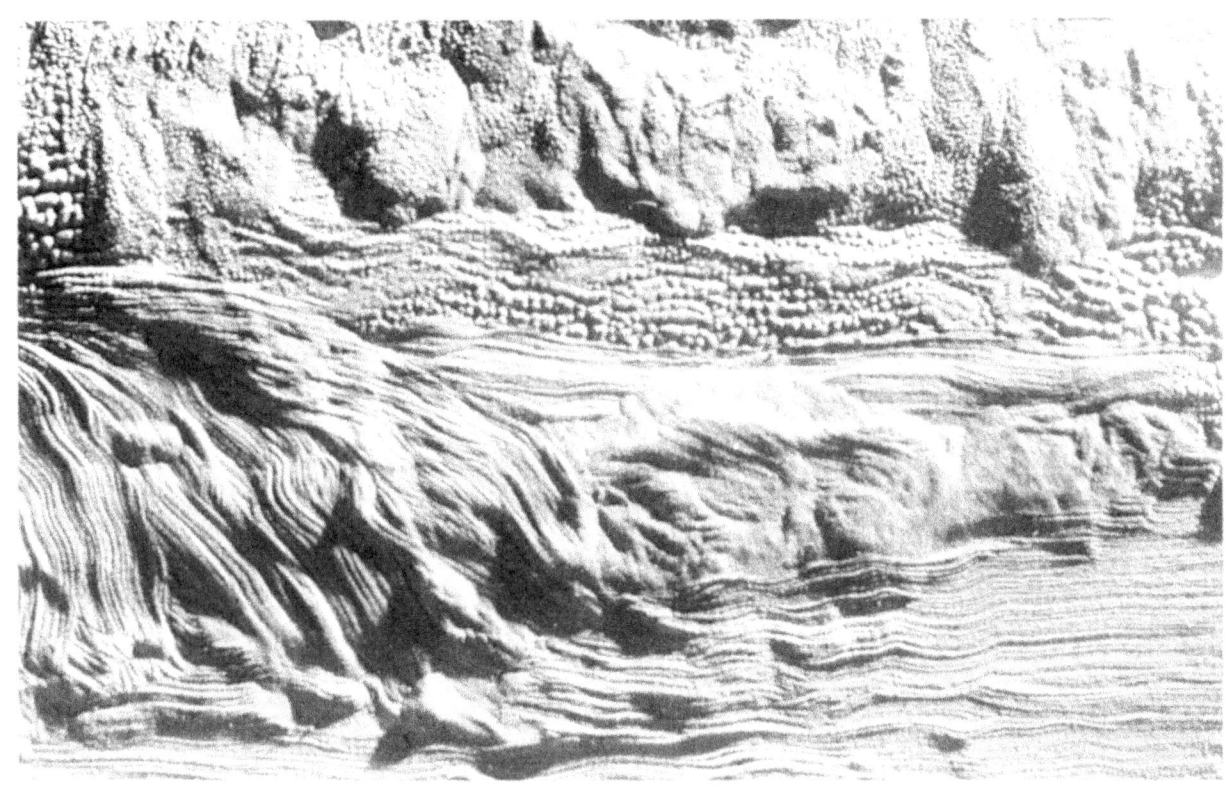

CLXXII

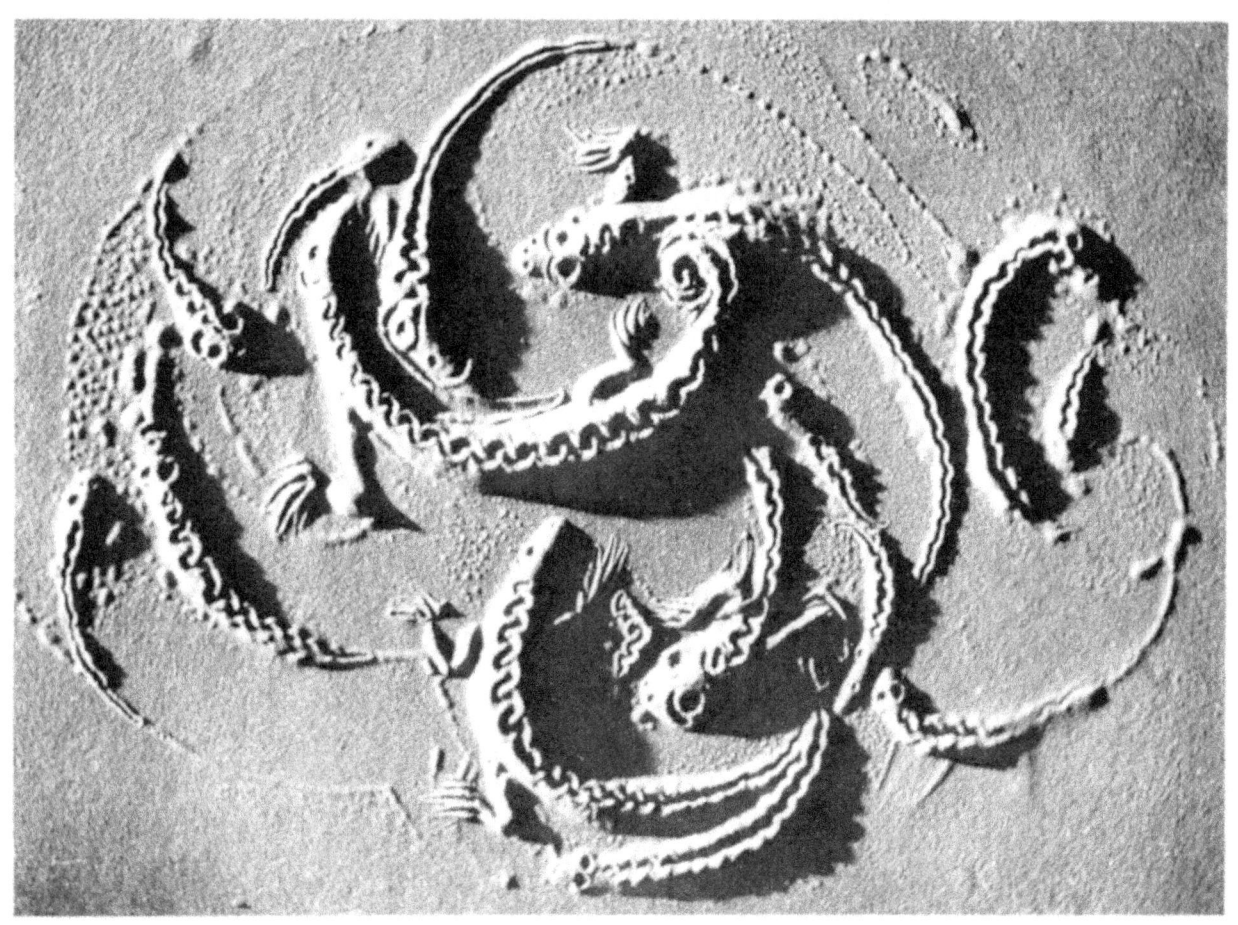

LI Lizards

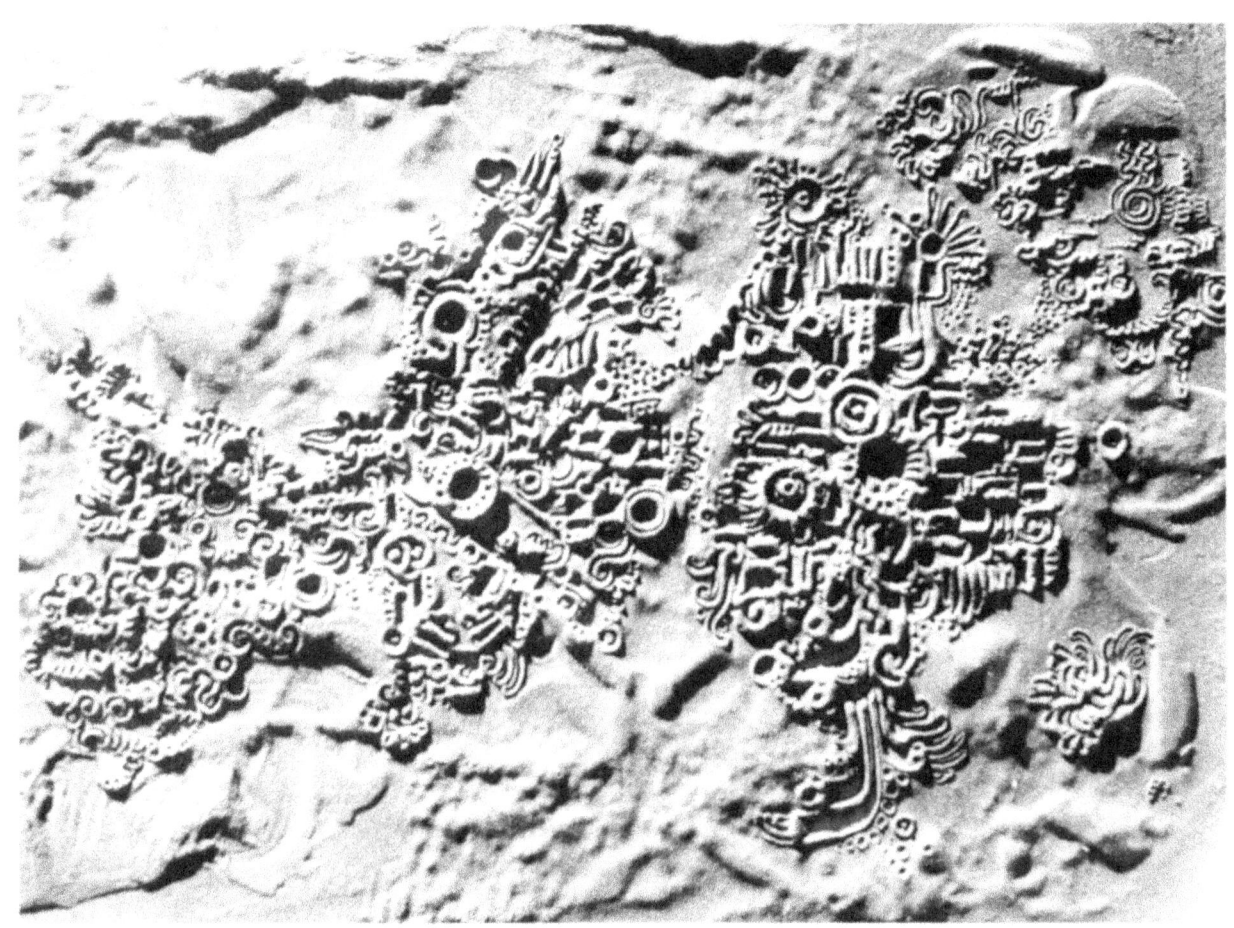

CLXIX

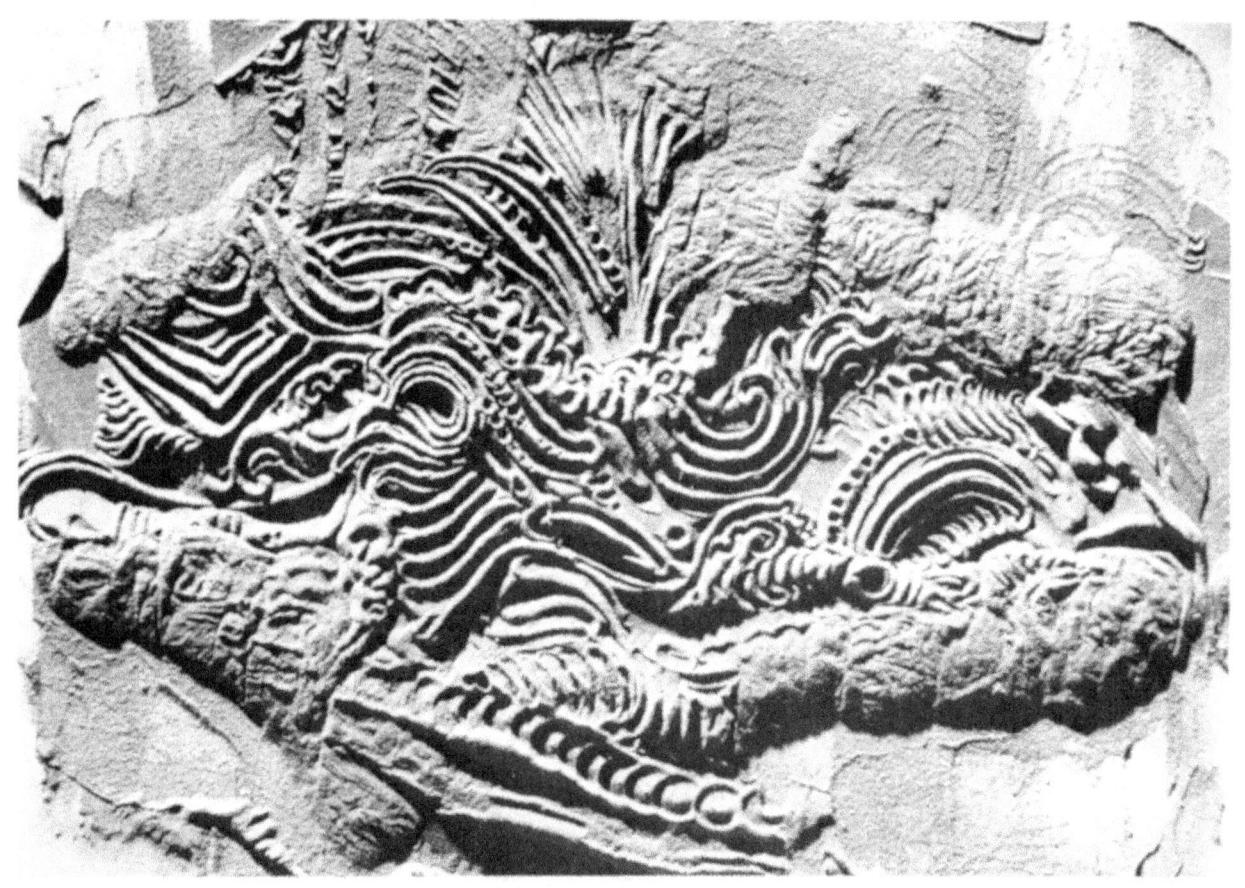

LVIII Ornamented Rock

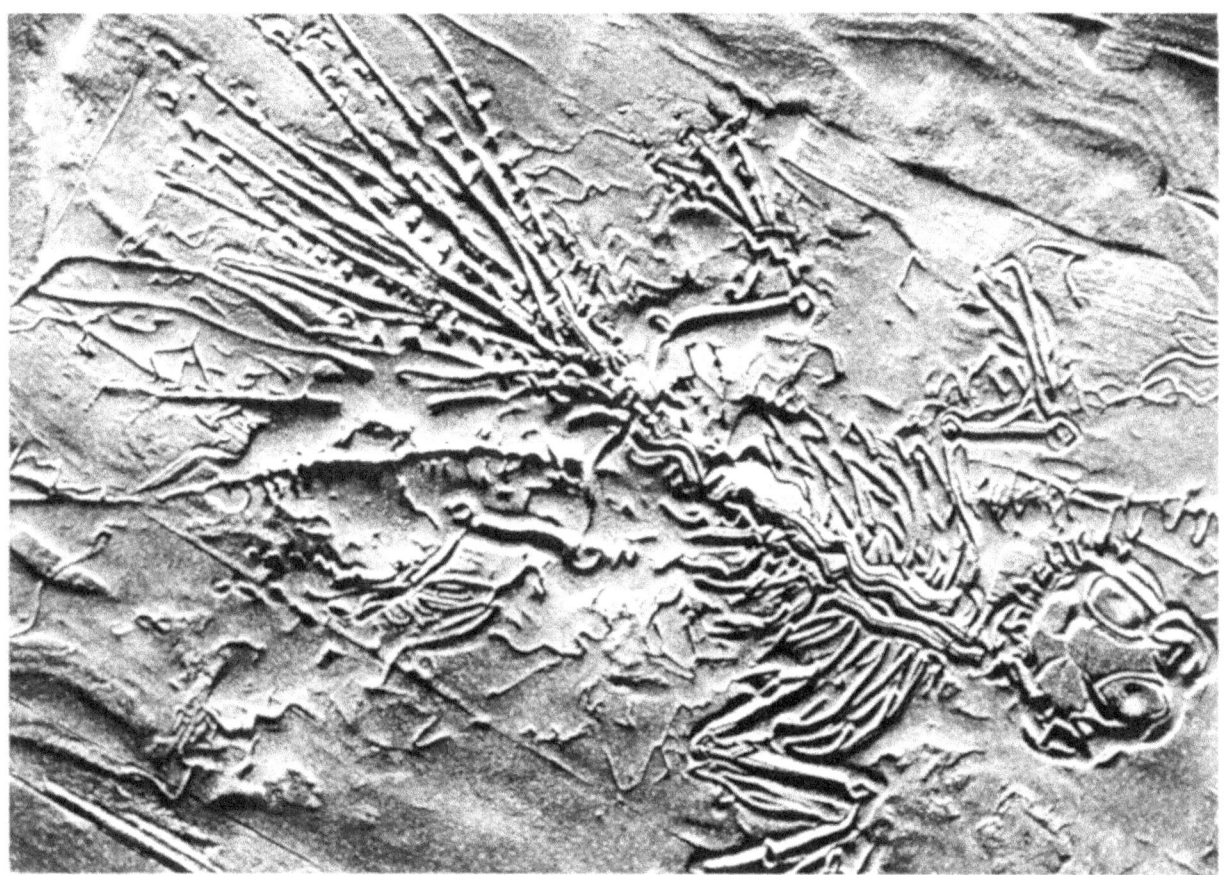

LXXIX Fossil

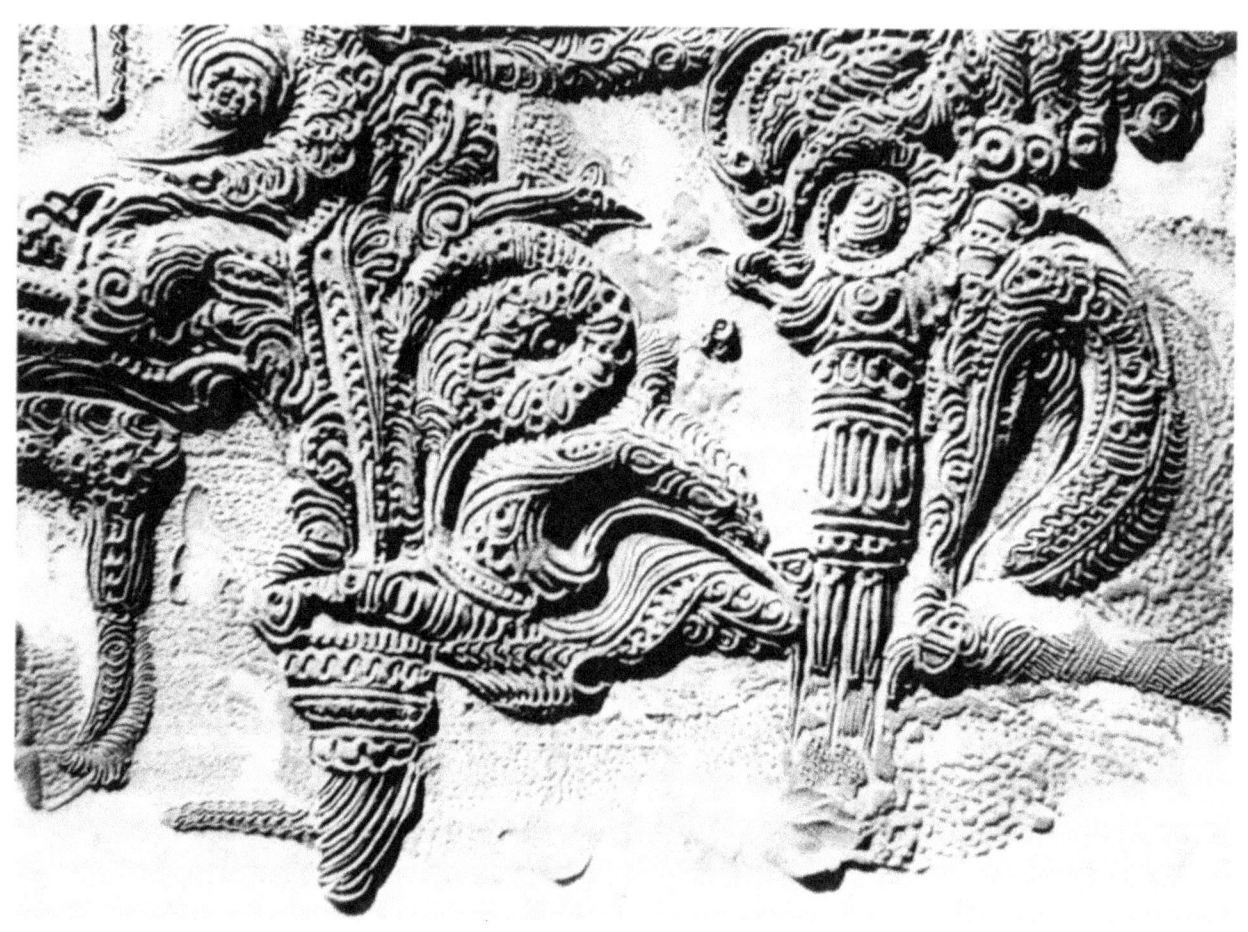

XXXII Torches

CLV Embroidery (opposite)

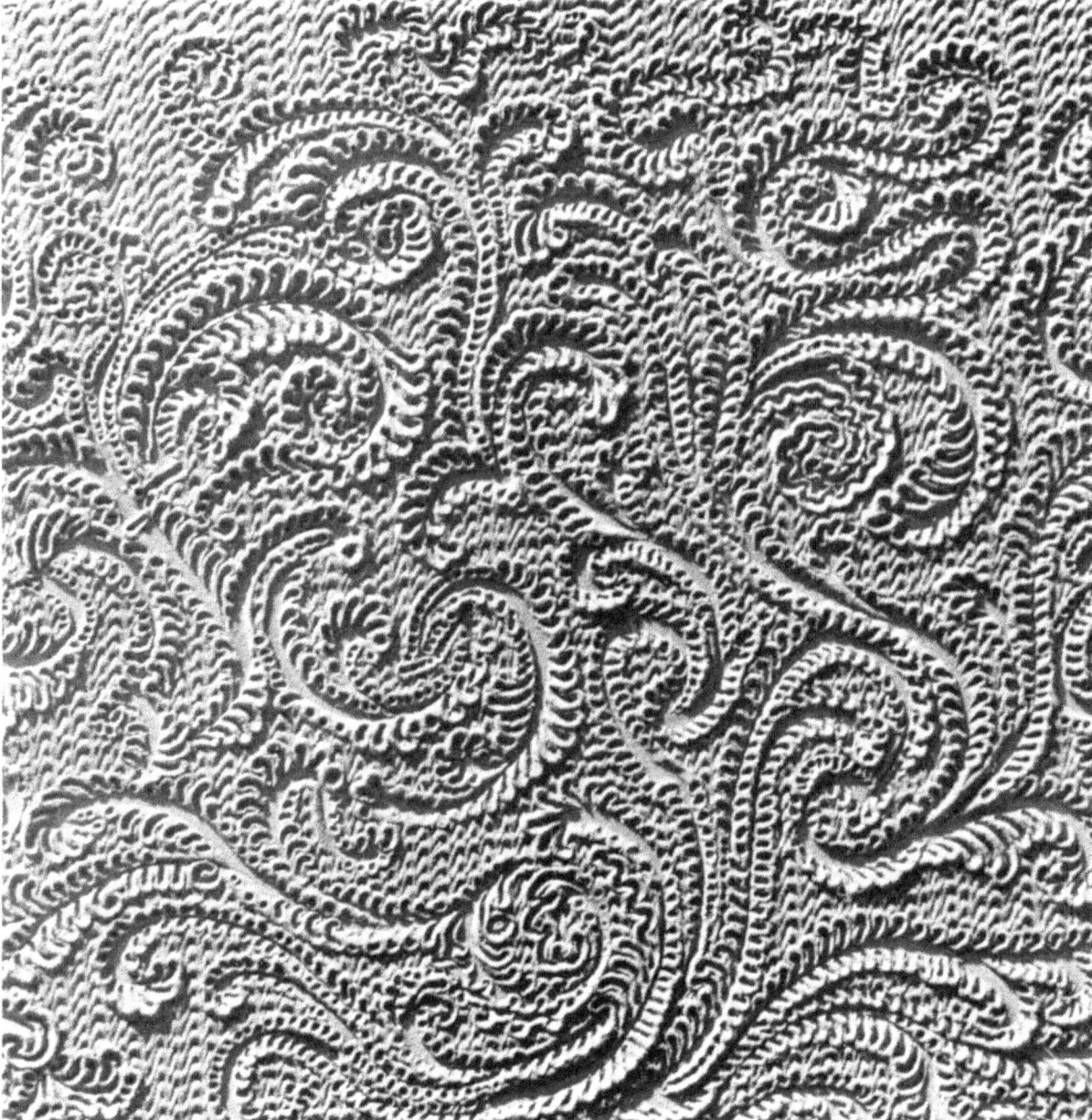

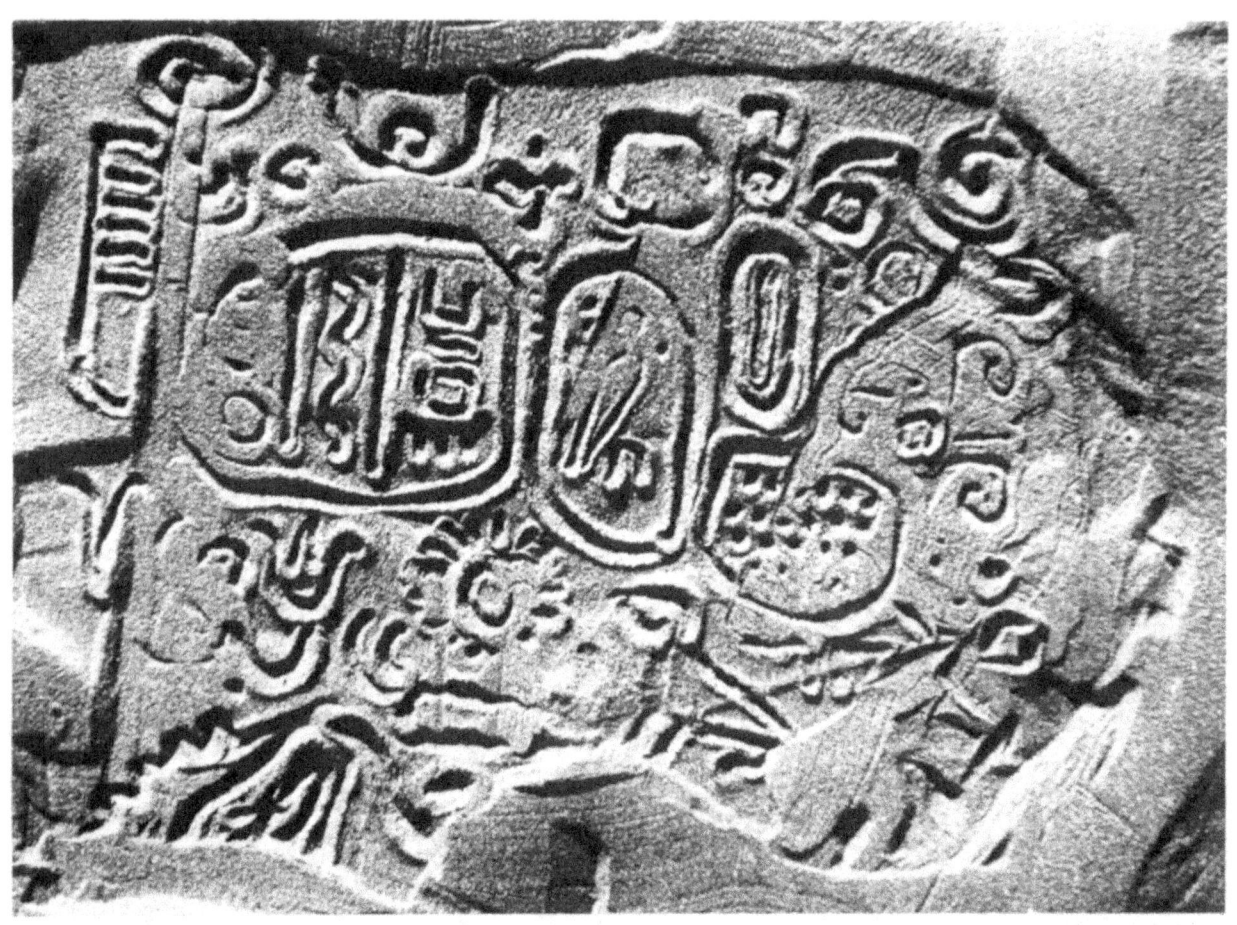

VIII Tabloid

CLXV (opposite)

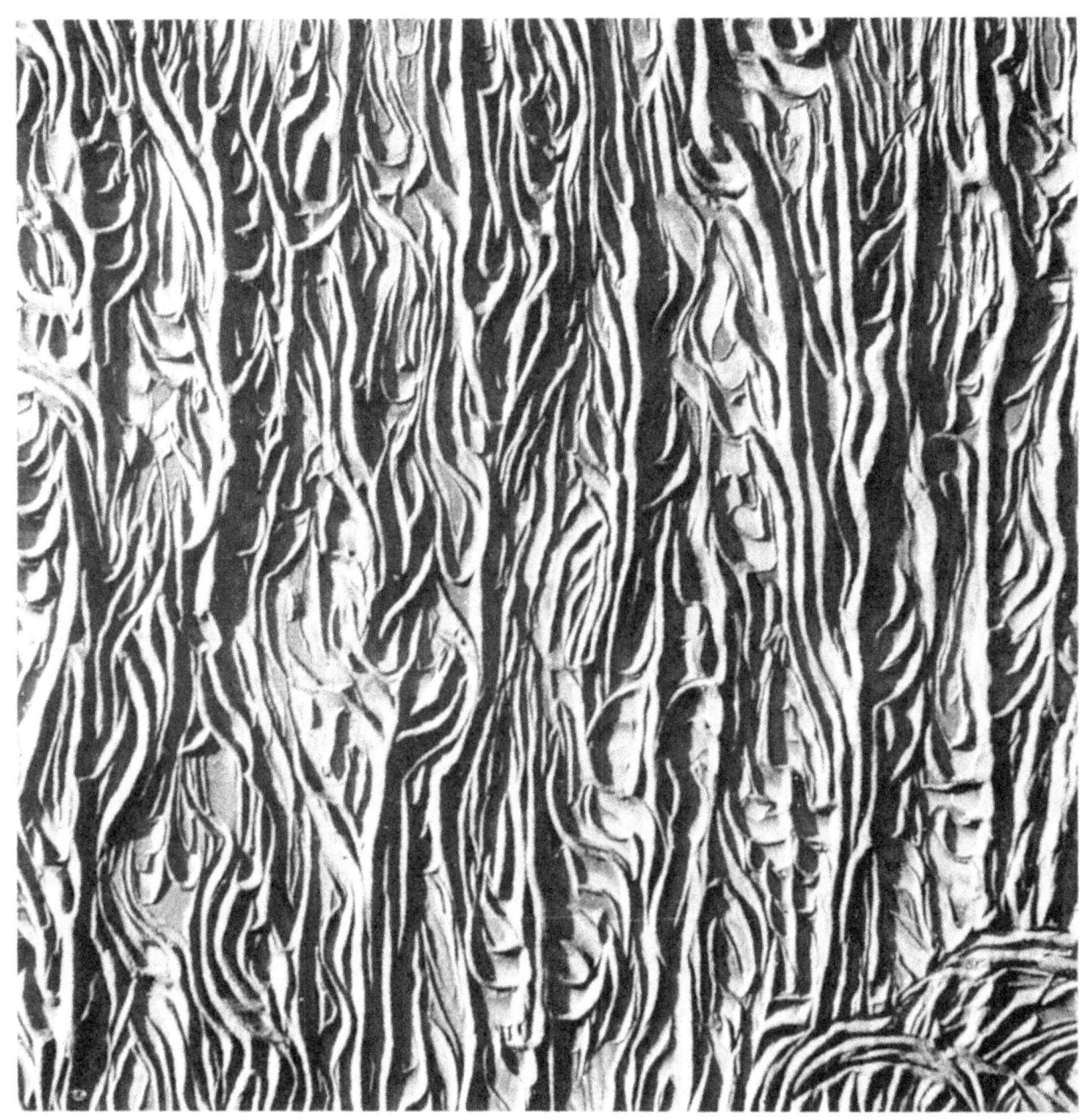

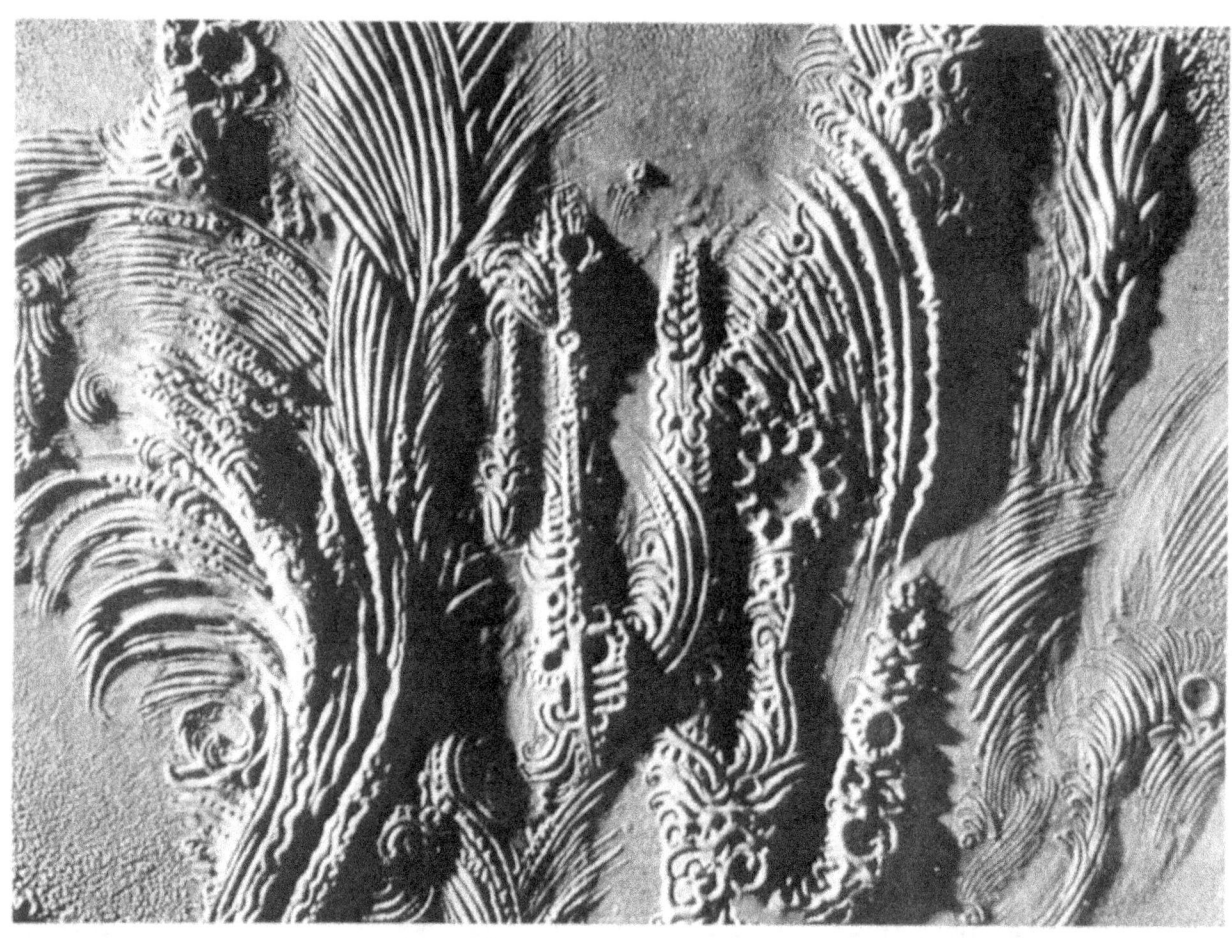

CLXXIII

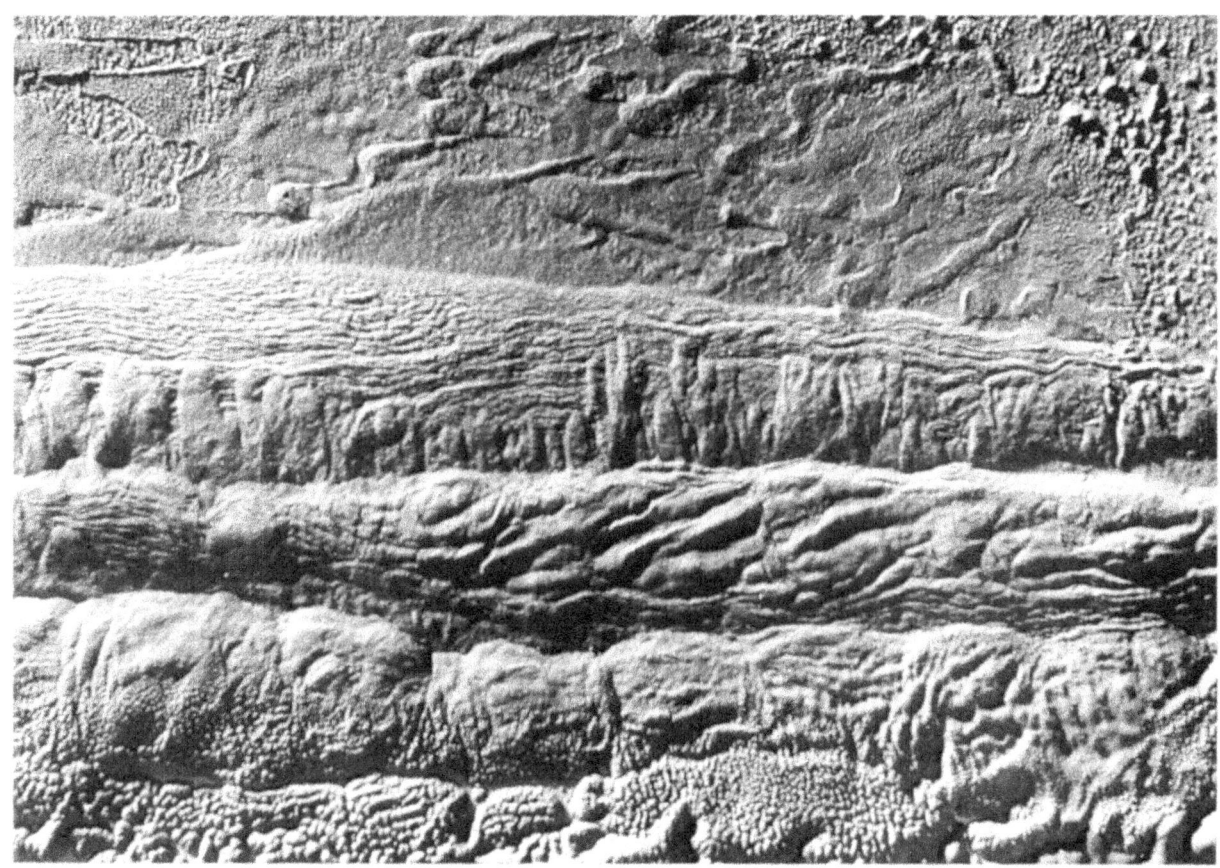

CLXVII

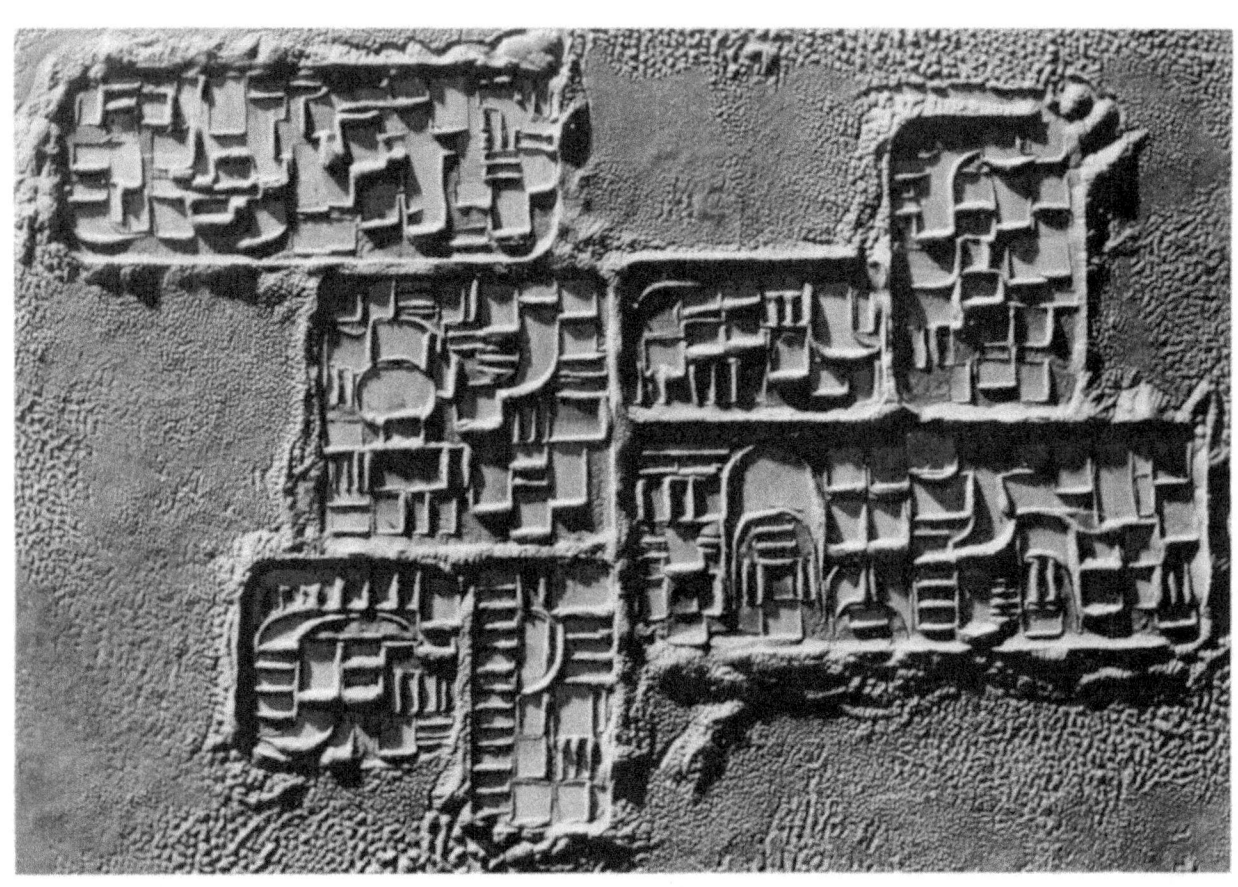

CLVIII Dwellings

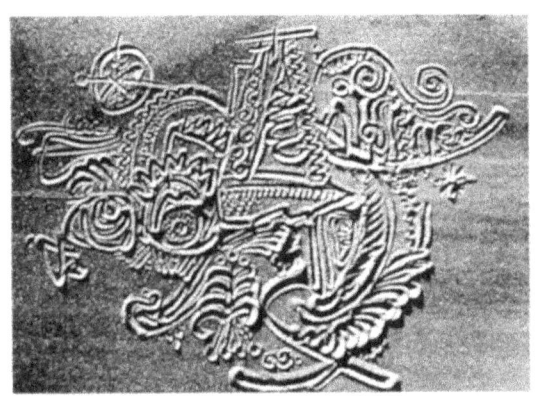

II

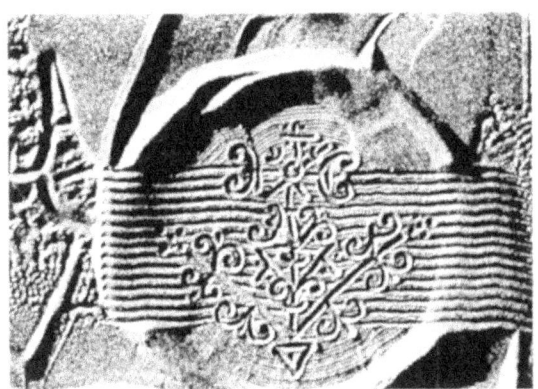

V

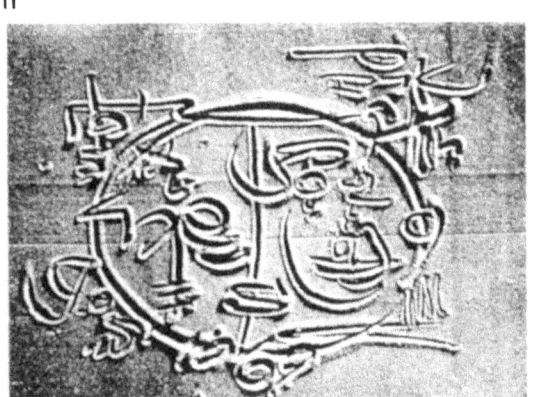

III

IV ▼

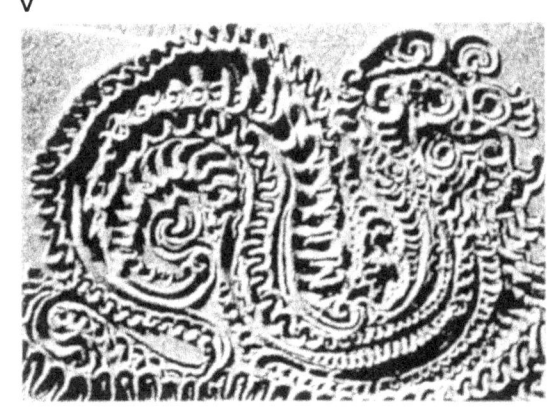

VI

IX ▼

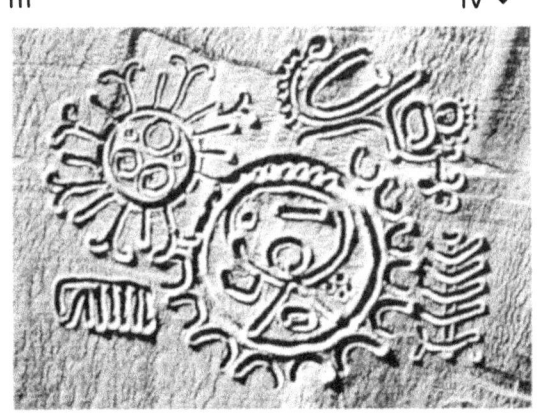

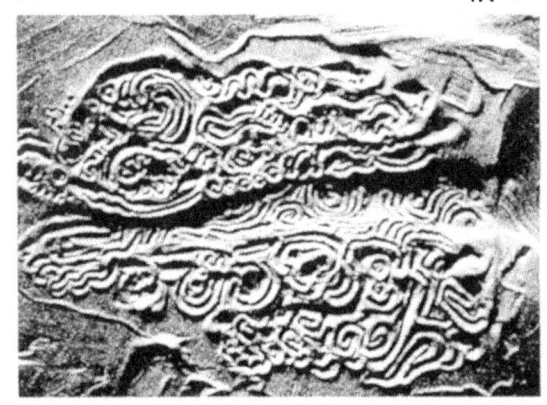

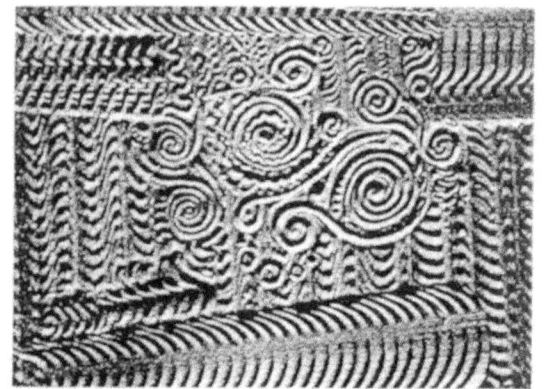

X Furrows and Spirals

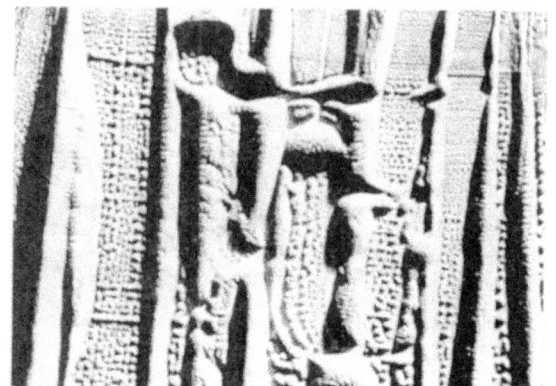

XVII Pillars

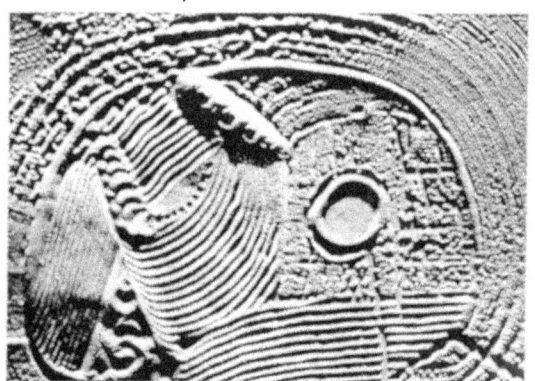

XIII   XV Dragon ▼

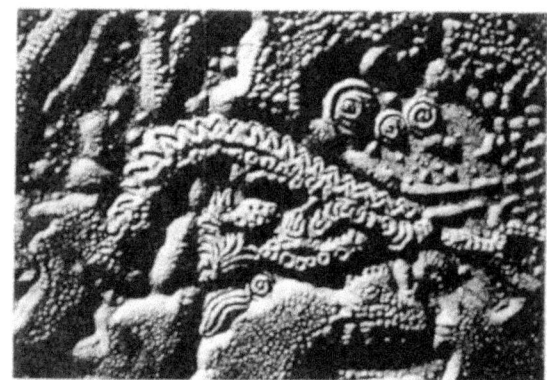

XVIII   XXI ▼

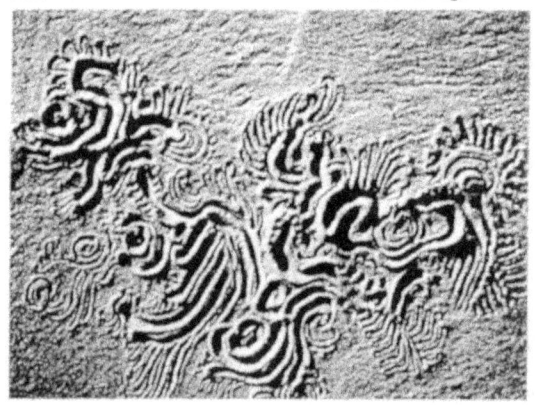

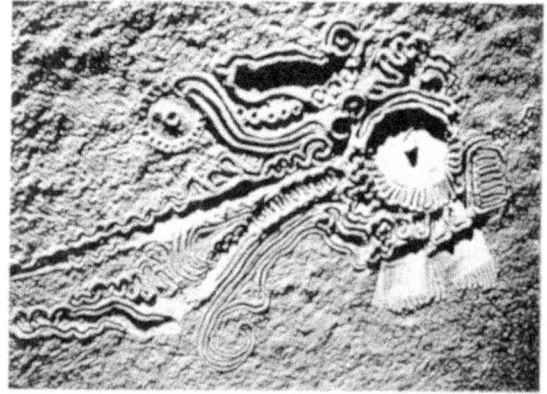

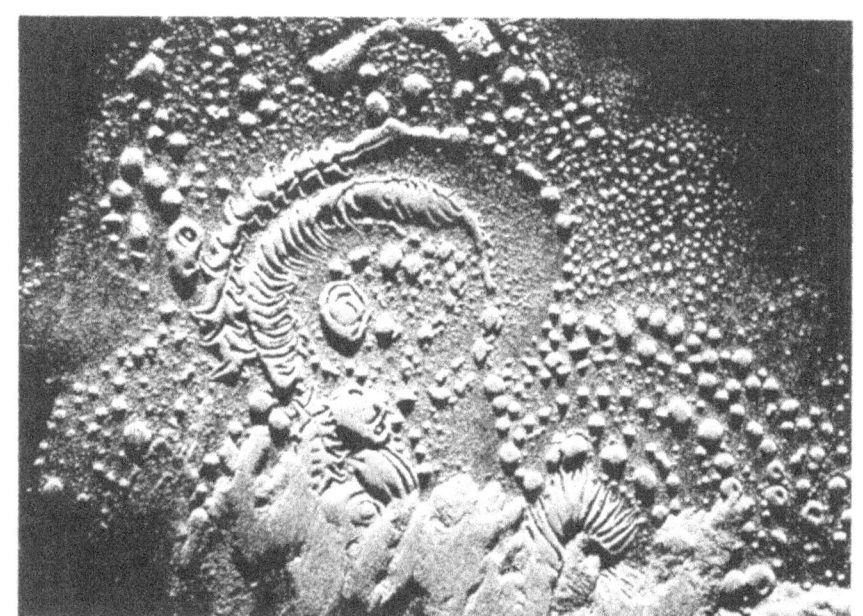

XXII July

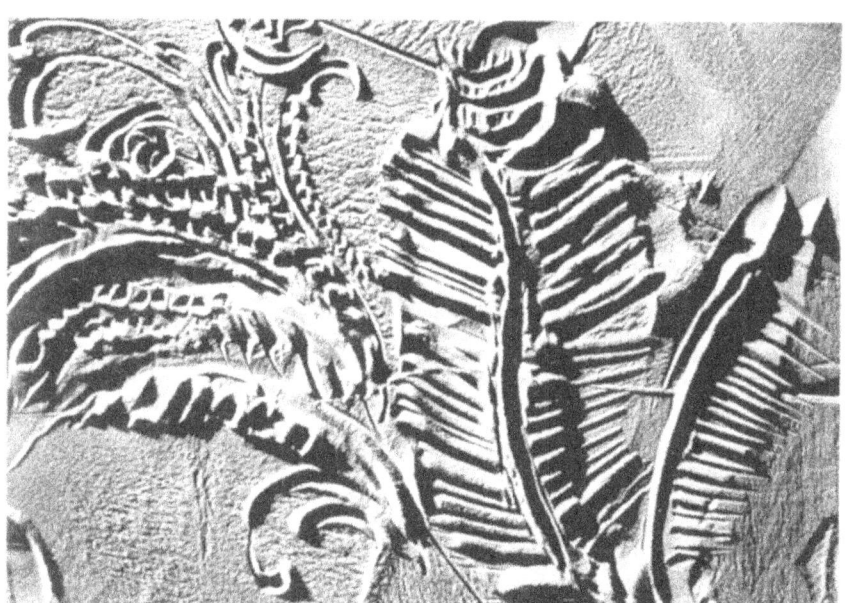

XXIV

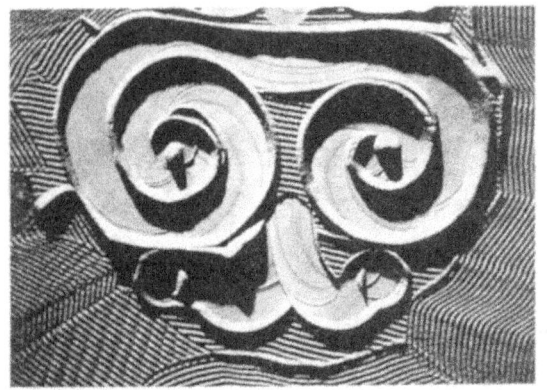

XXV

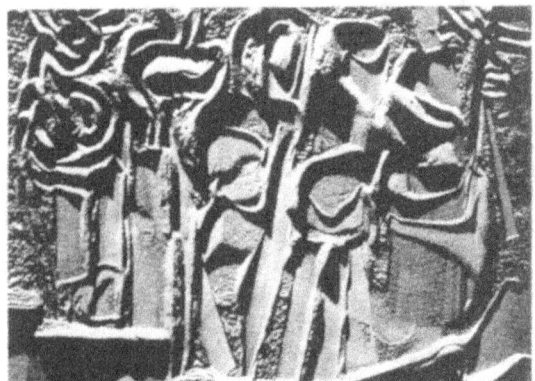

XXVIII Serenade   XXXI ▼

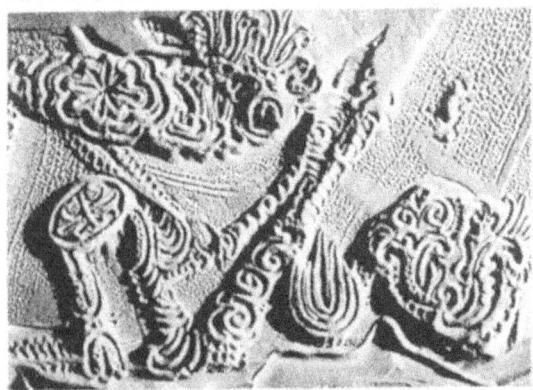

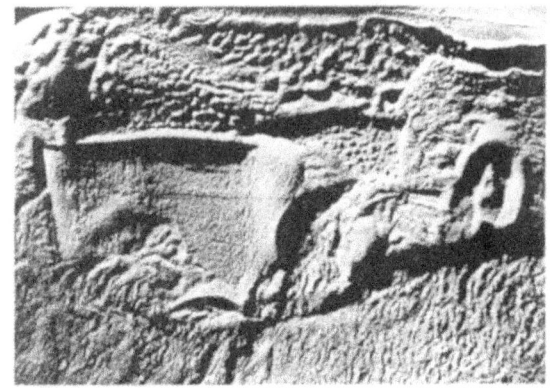

XXXIV

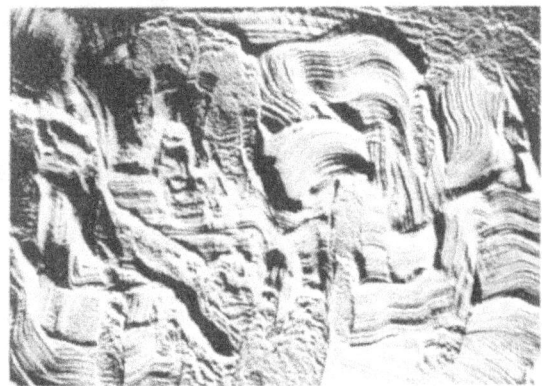

XXXV   XXXVII ▼

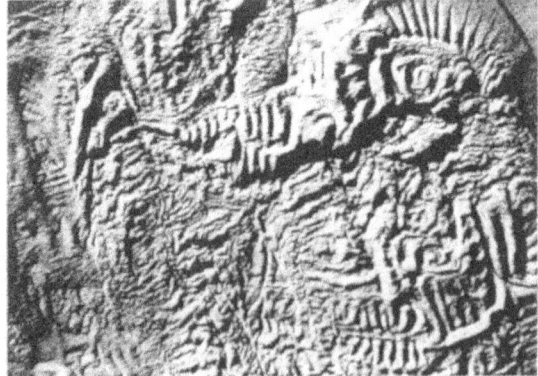

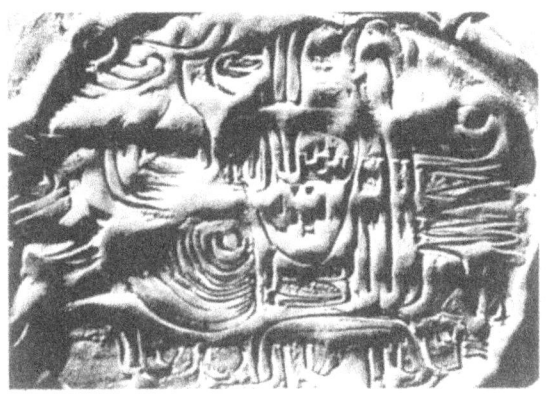

XXXVIII

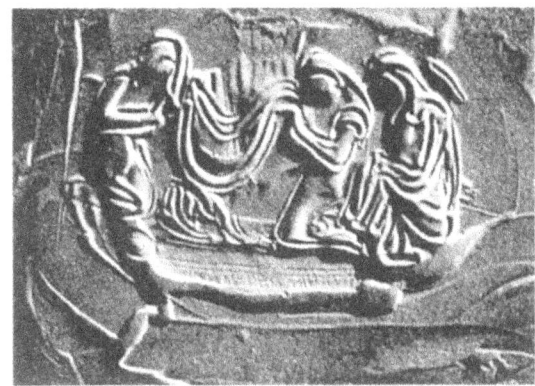

XLIII

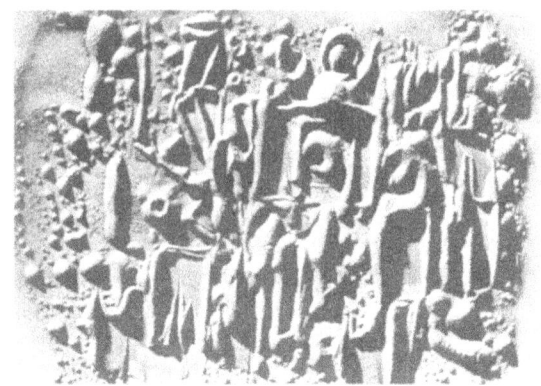

XLI Sermon

XLII ▼

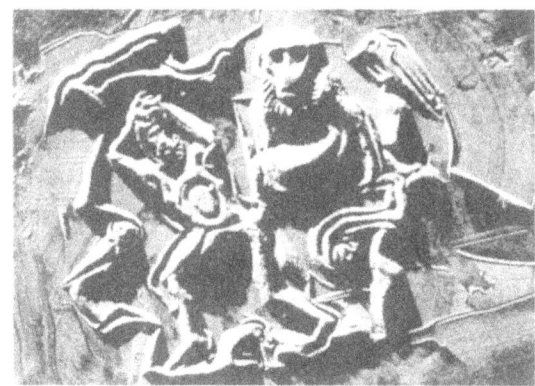

XLIV

XLV Horsemen ▼

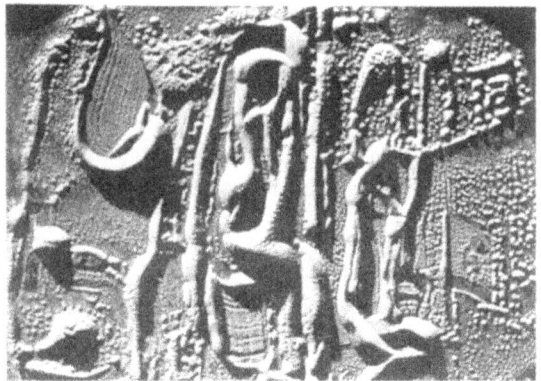

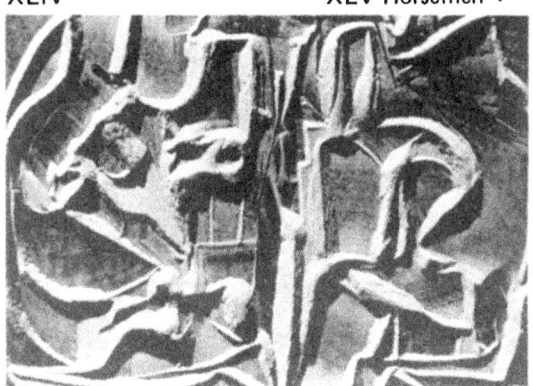

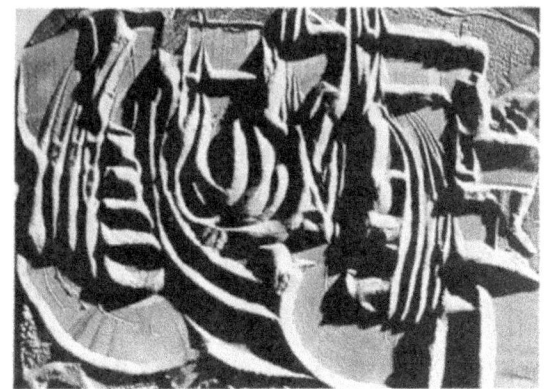

XLVI

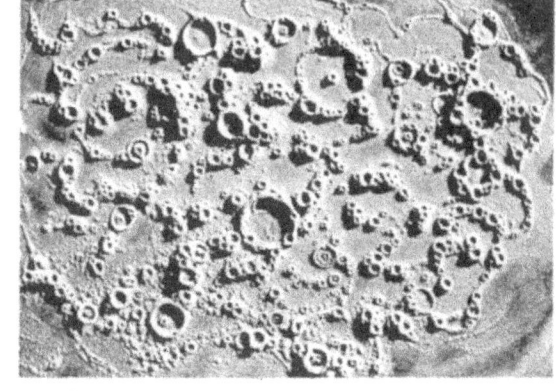

XLIX

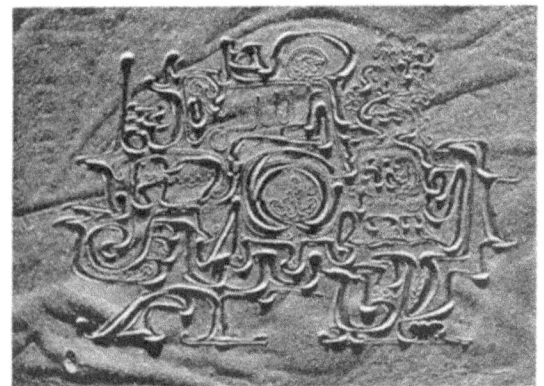

XLVII Five Thirteen

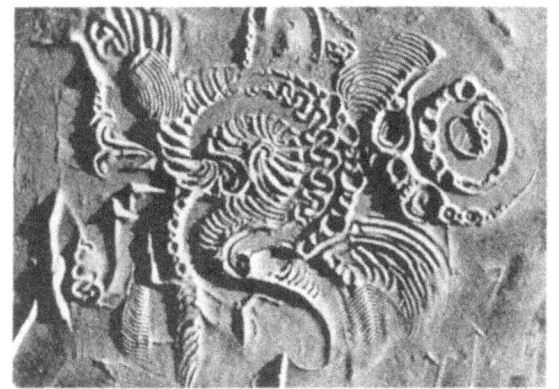

XLVIII ▼

L   LII ▼

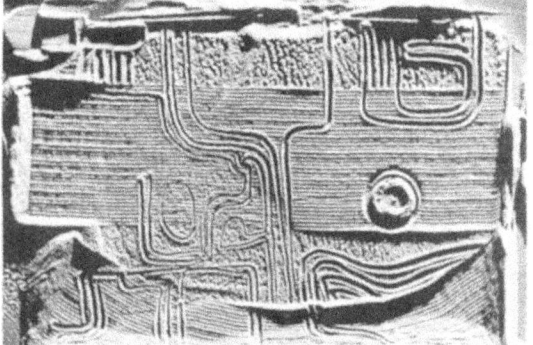

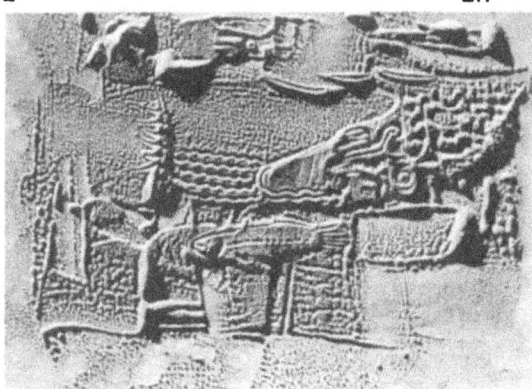

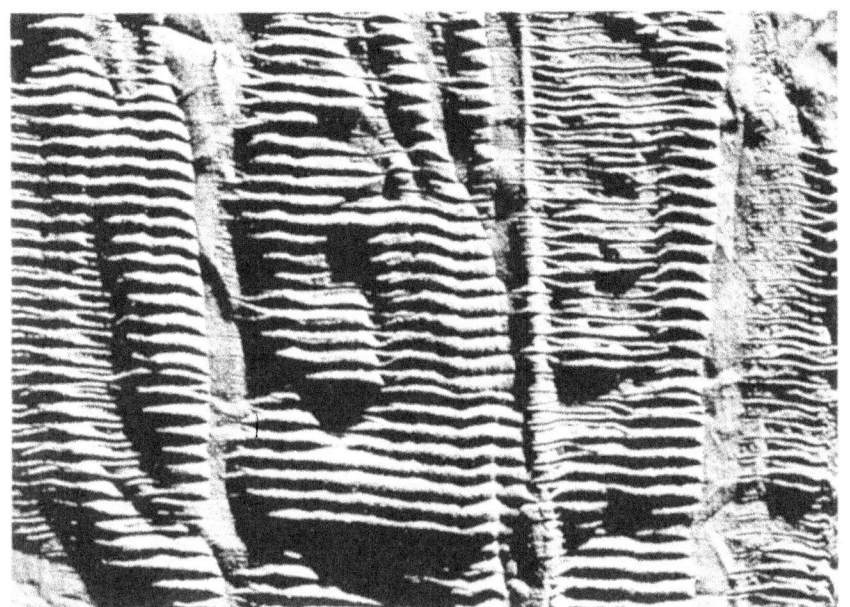

LIII

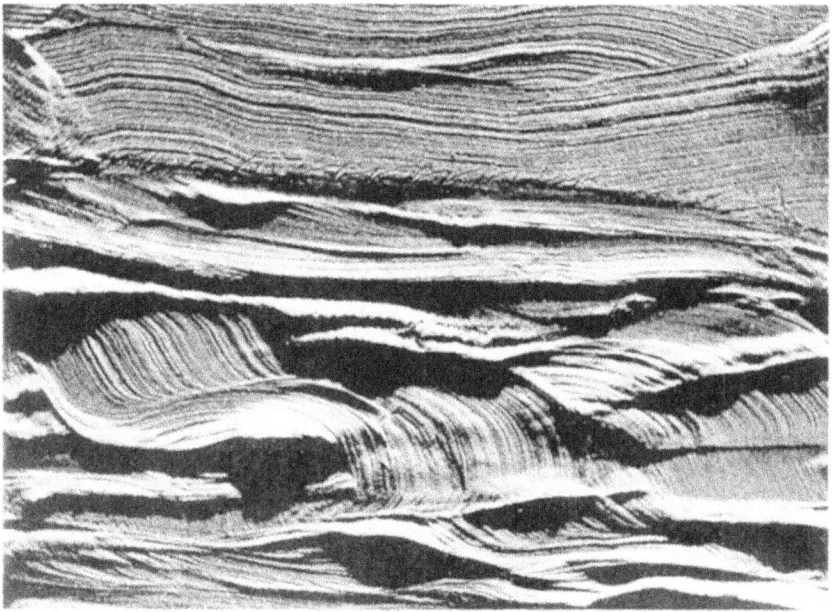

LIV Waves

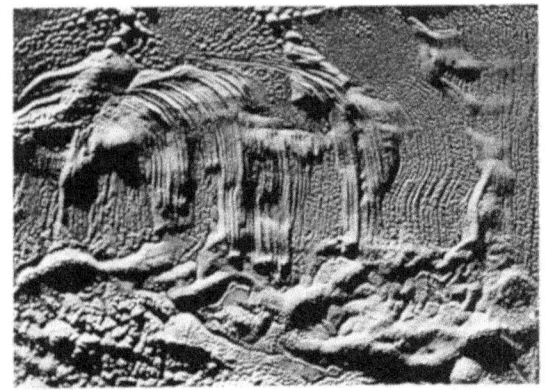

LV Winter

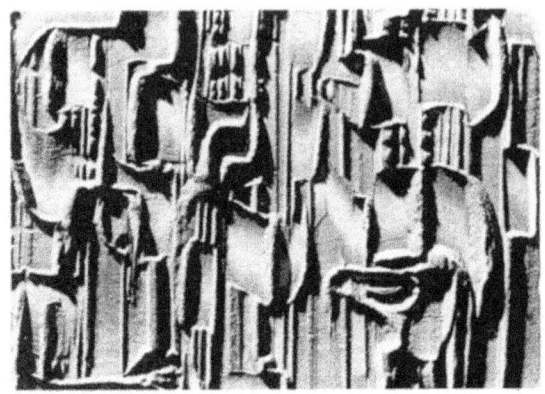

LXI

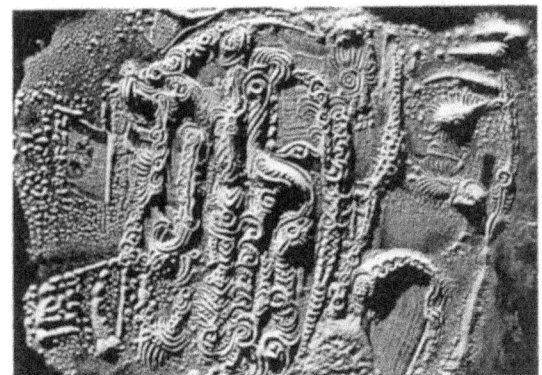

LVII   LIX Fireplace ▼

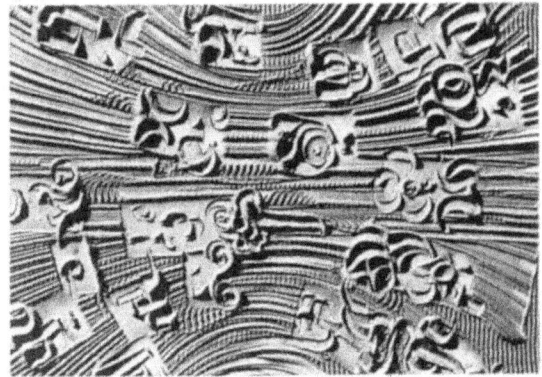

LXII   LXIII Palace ▼

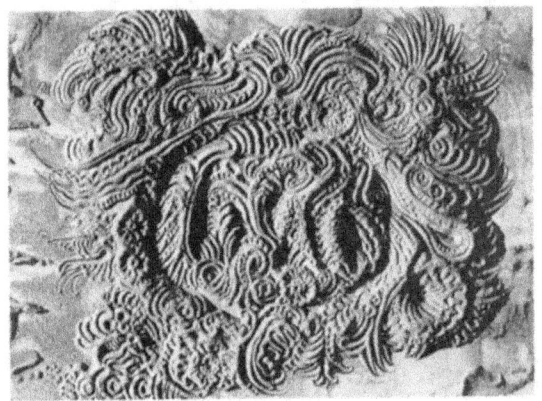

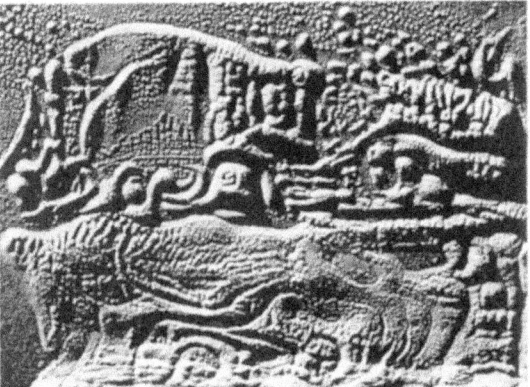

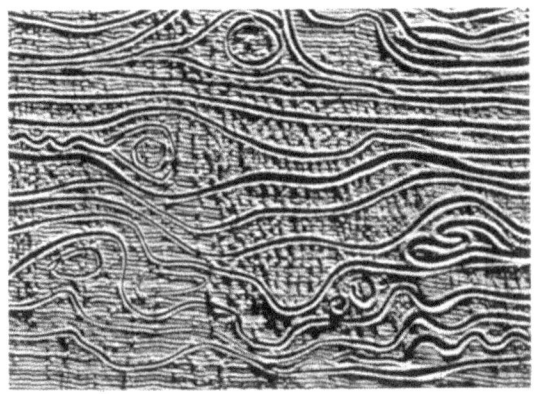

LXIV

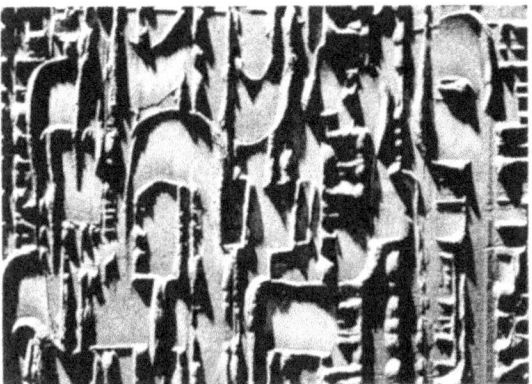

LXVII Facade West

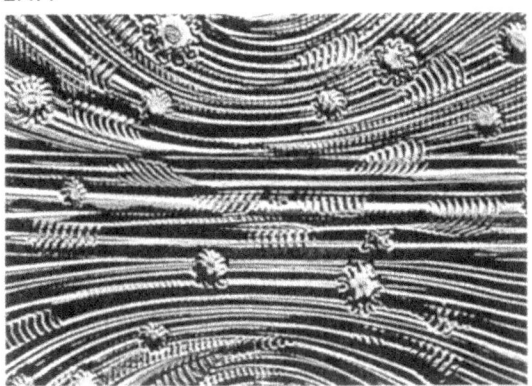

LXV

LXVI ▼

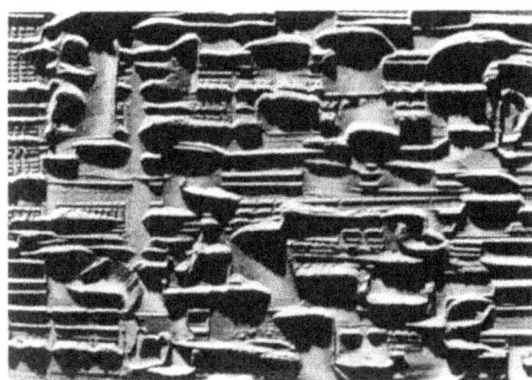

LXVIII

LXIX ▼

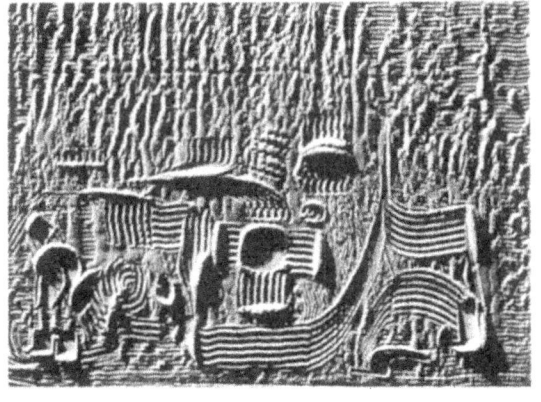

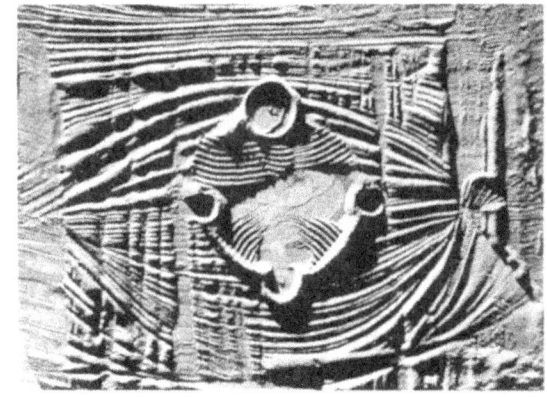

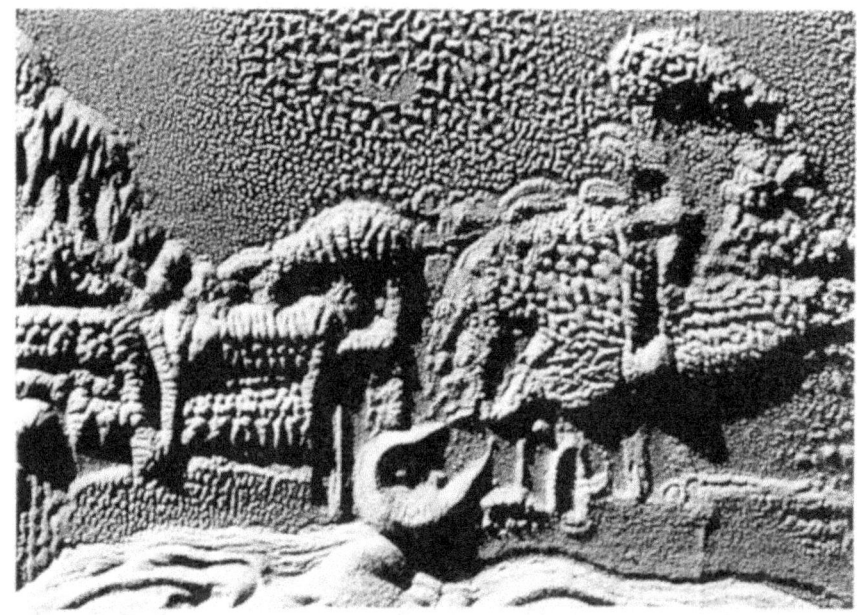

LXXI

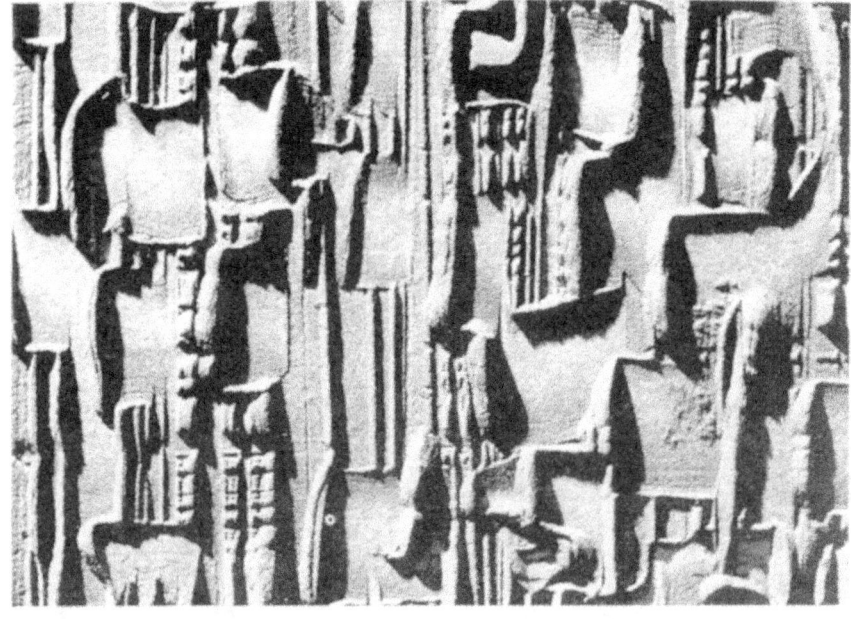

LXXII Facade East

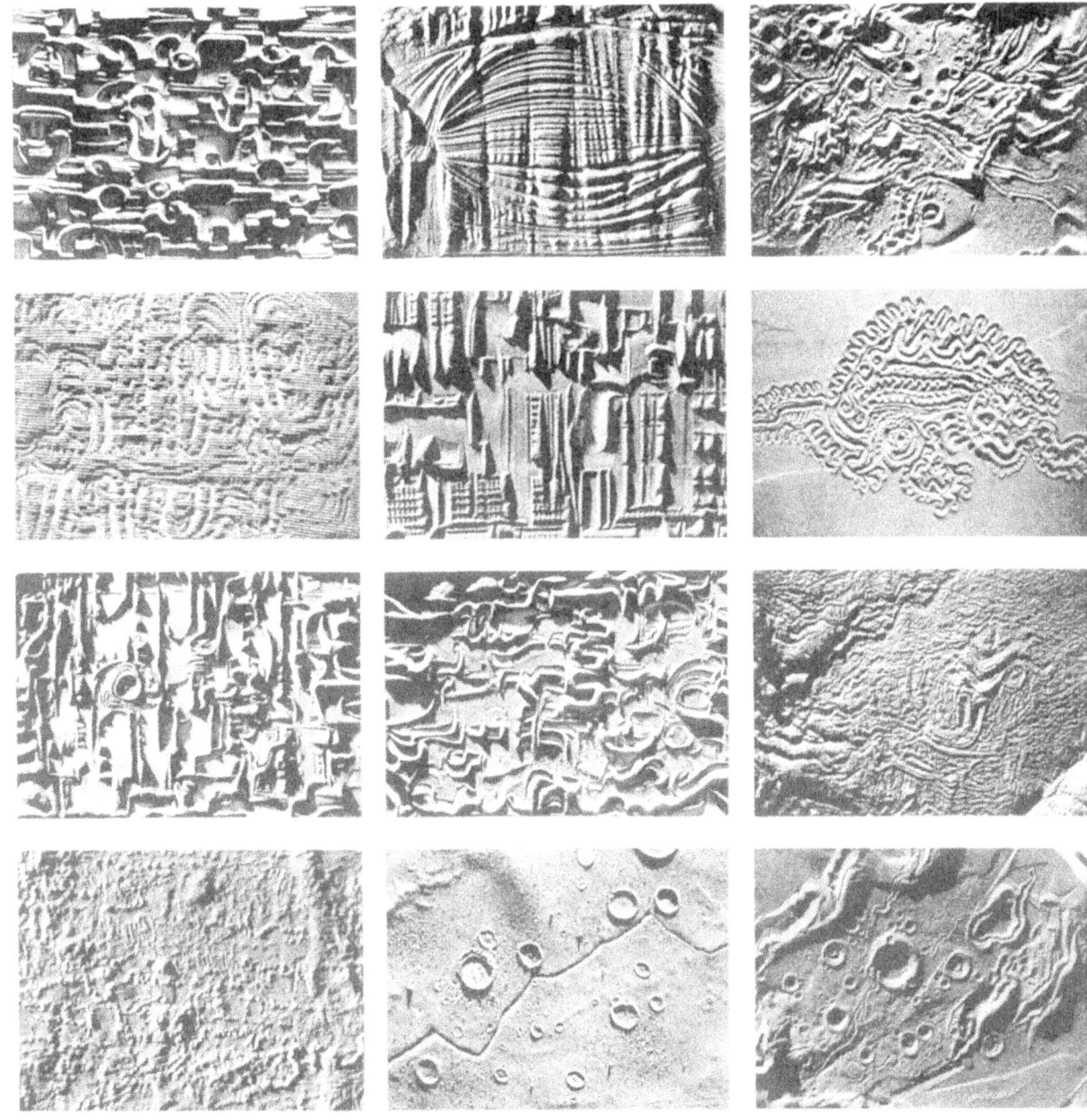

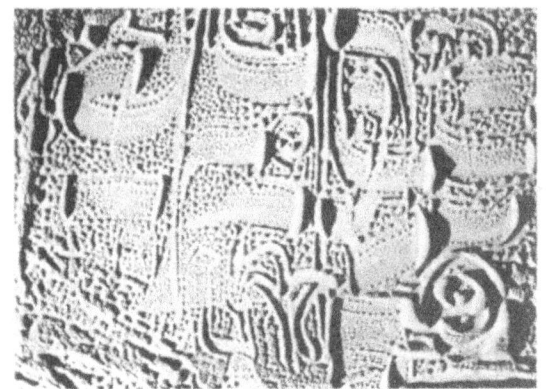

LXXXVII

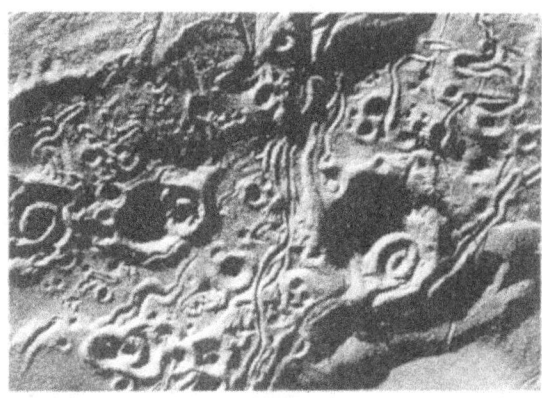

XC

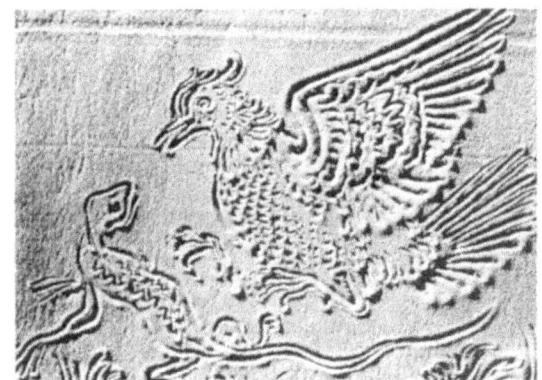

LXXXVIII   LXXXIX ▼

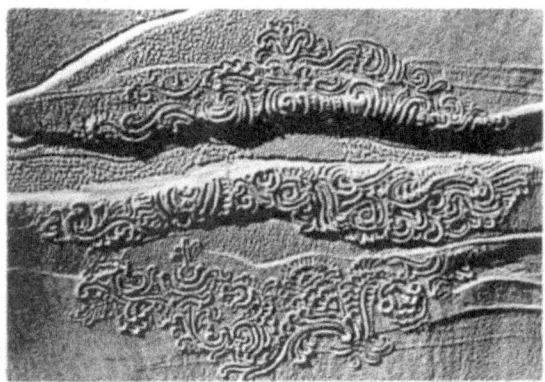

XCI Groove   XCII ▼

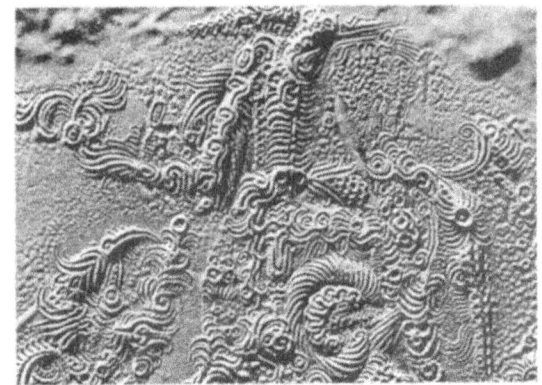

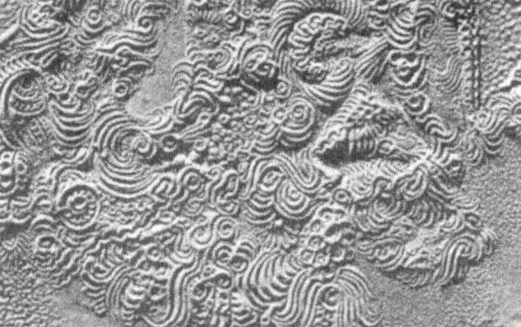

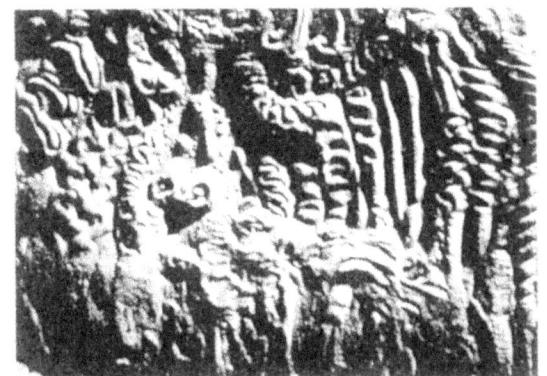

XCIII

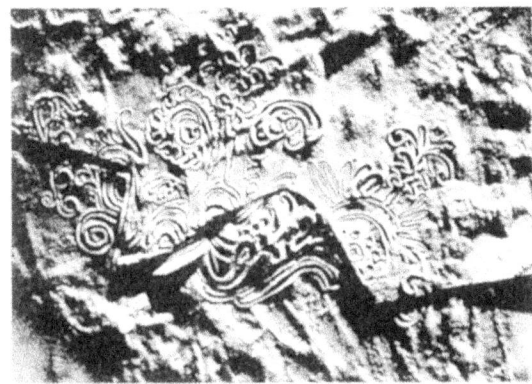

XCVI

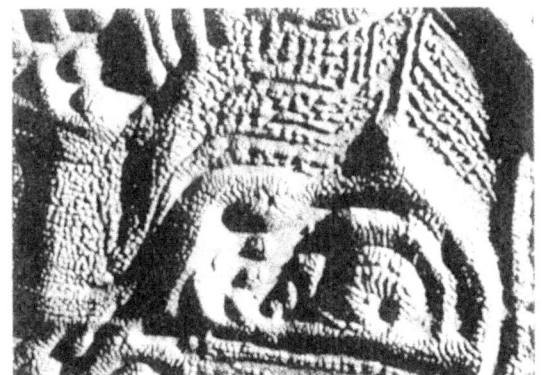

XCIV

XCV ▼

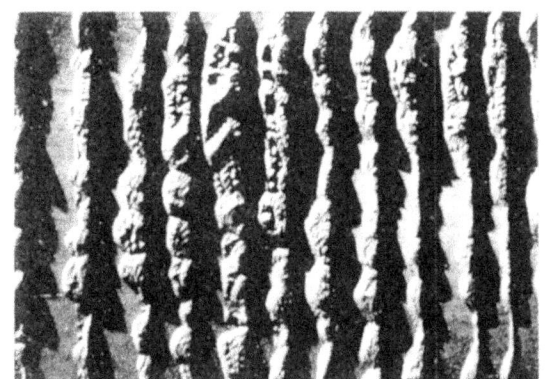

XCVII

XCVIII ▼

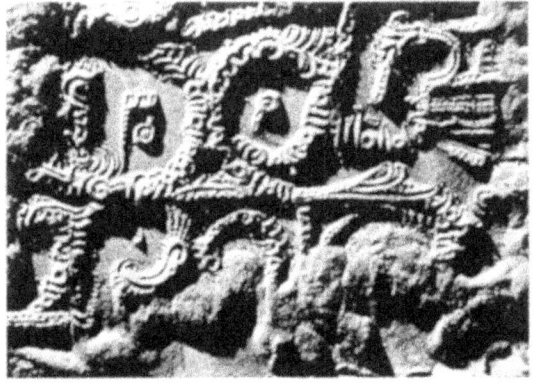

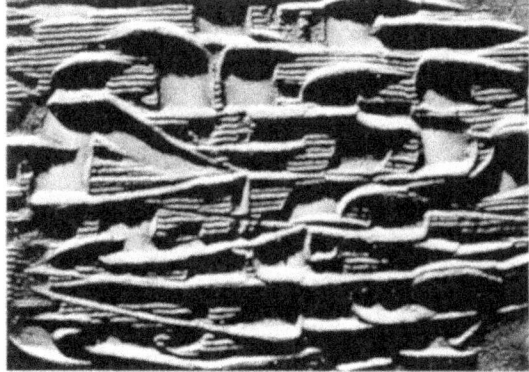

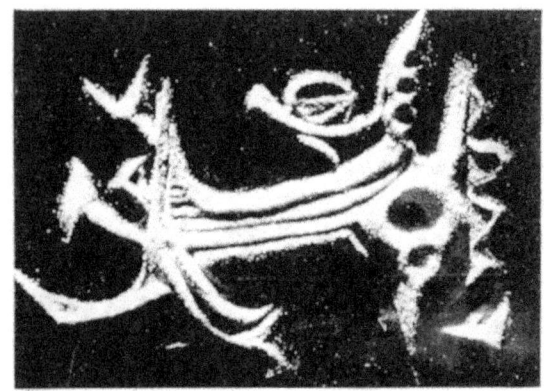

XCIX

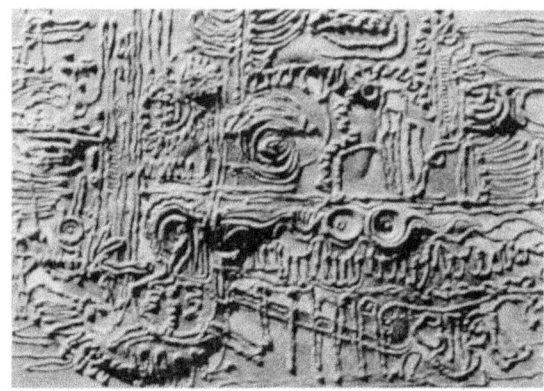

CII Festival in Venice

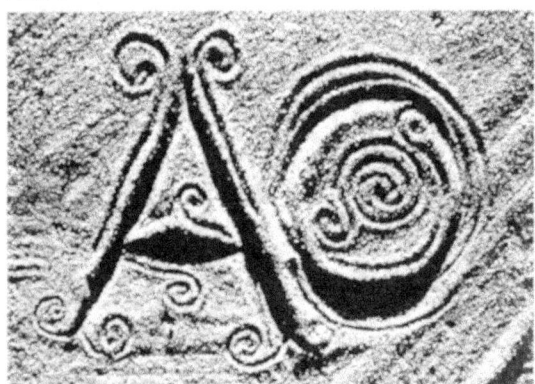

C   CI Trowel Work ▼

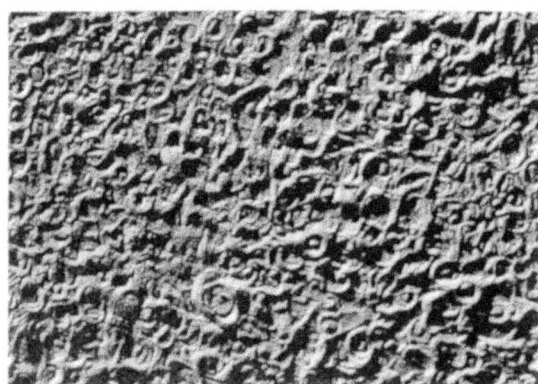

CIII   CIV Facade South ▼

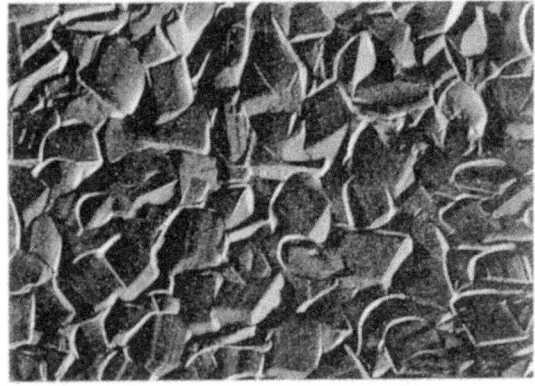

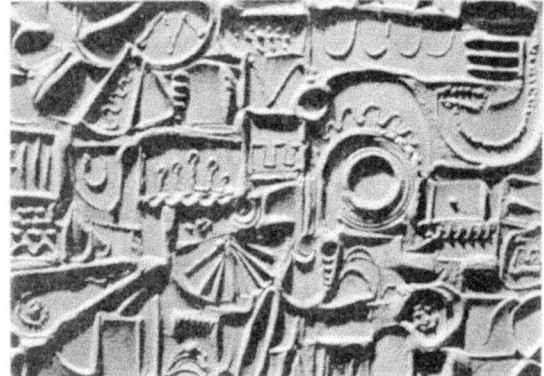

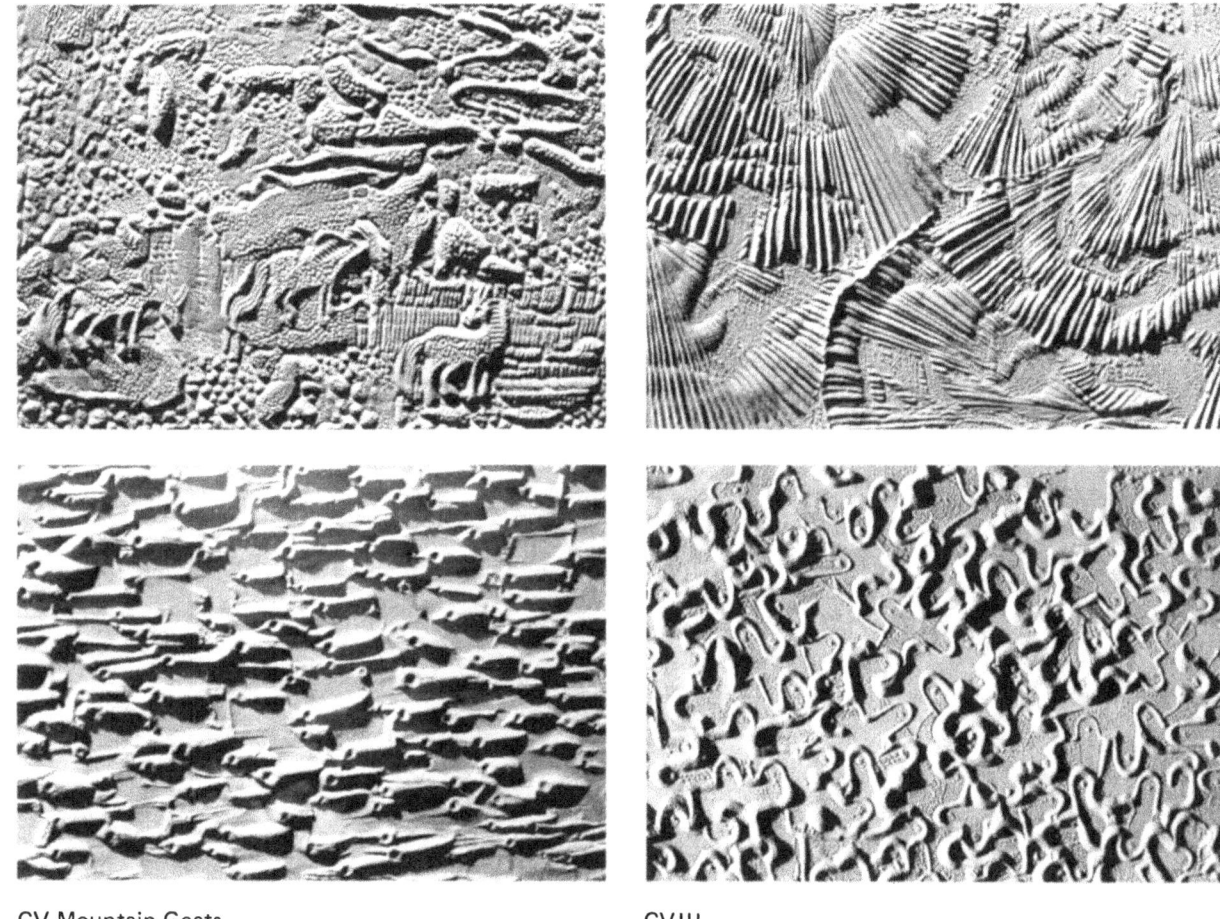

CV Mountain Goats

CVII

CVIII

CIX Dumplings

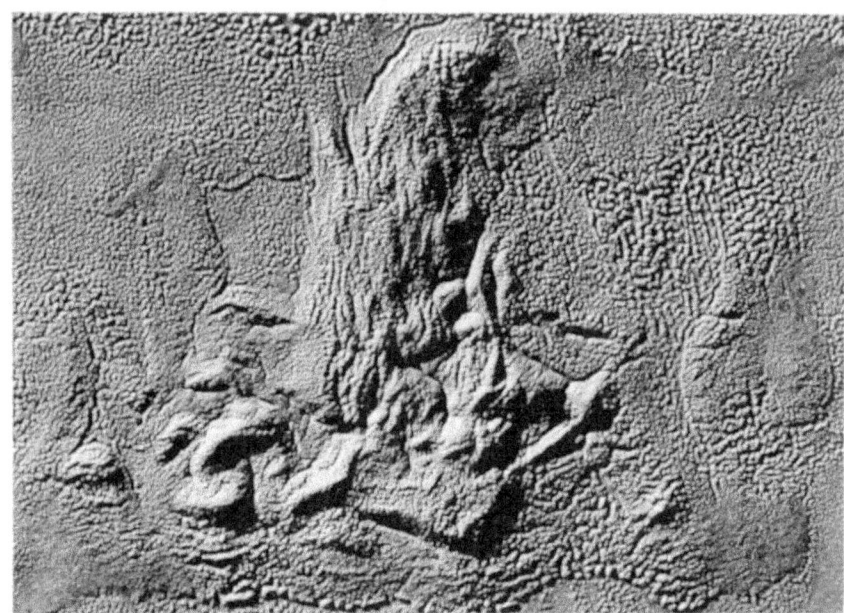

CX Flame

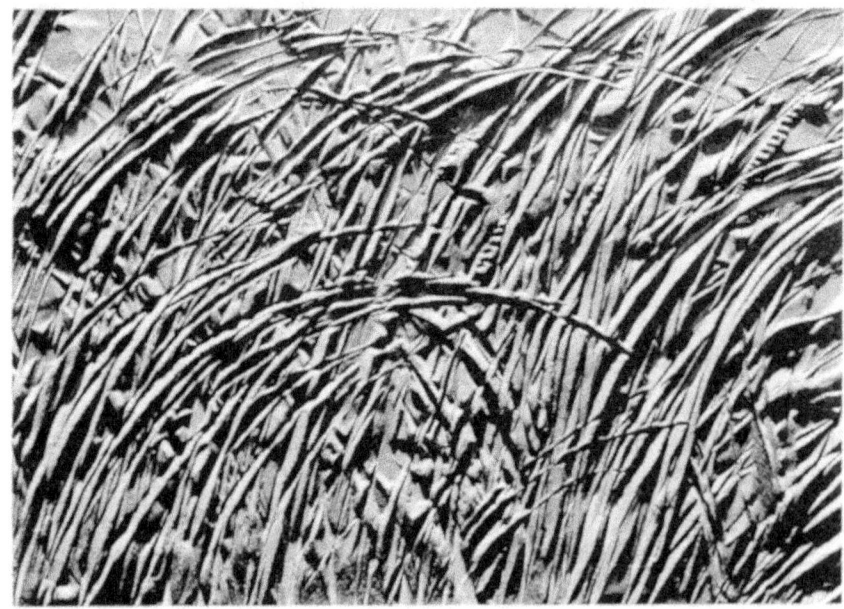

CXII Grass

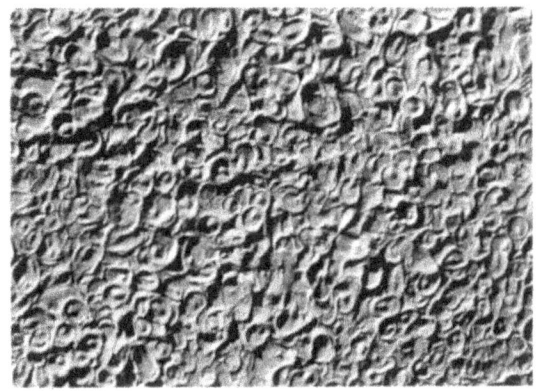

CXIII

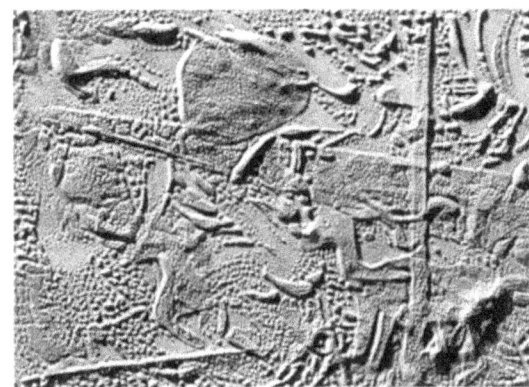

CXVI Corral

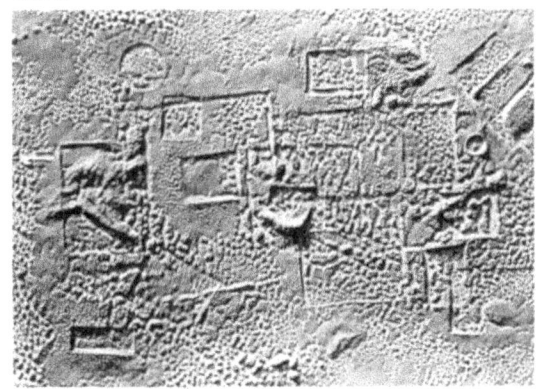

CXIV Archeological Site　　　　　　　　CXV ▼

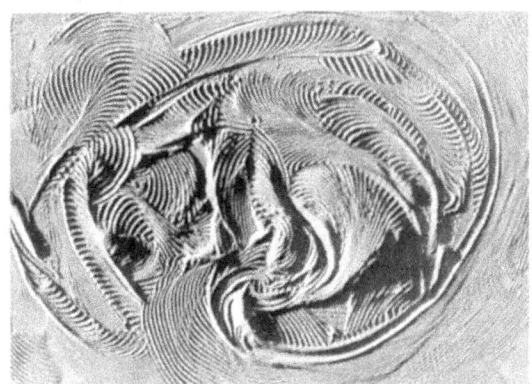

CXVIII Chain Traces　　　　CXIX Cleopatra ▼

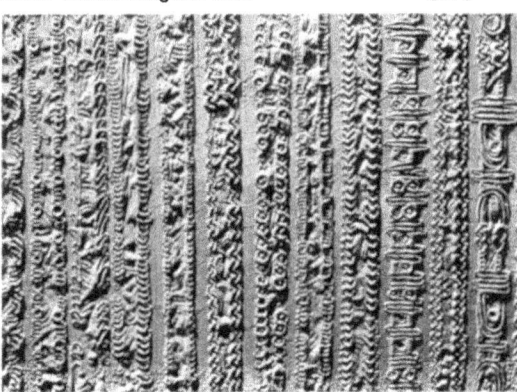

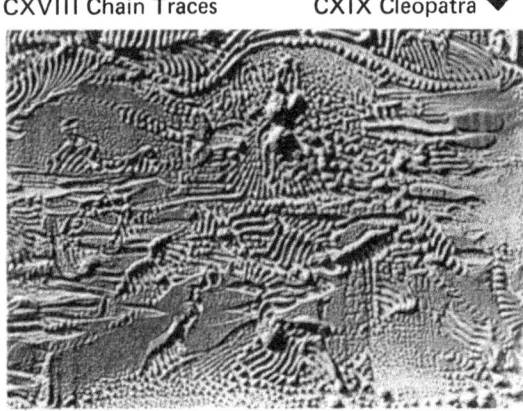

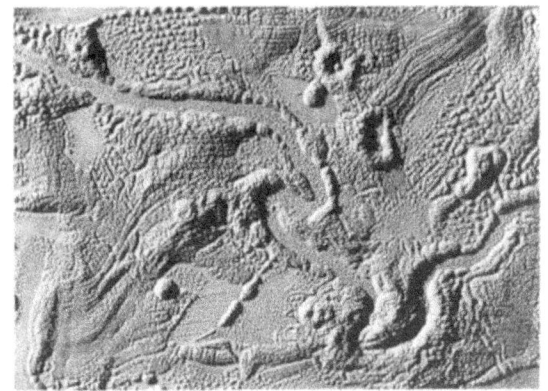

CXX

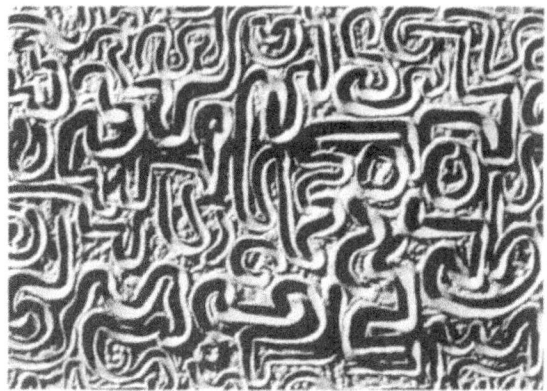

CXXIII

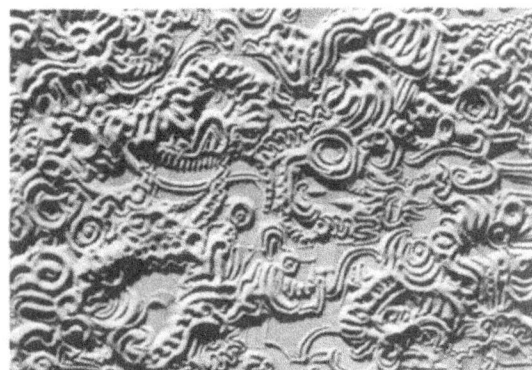

CXXI Gingerbread   CXXII Facade North ▼

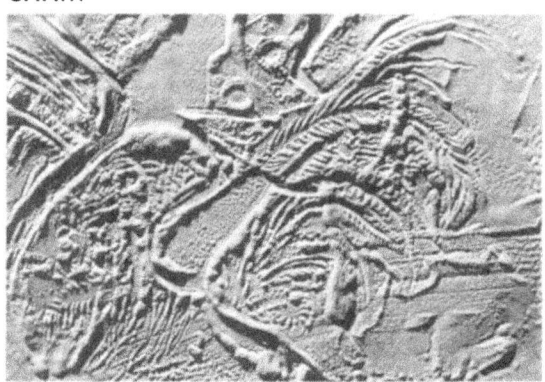

CXXIV September   CXXV ▼

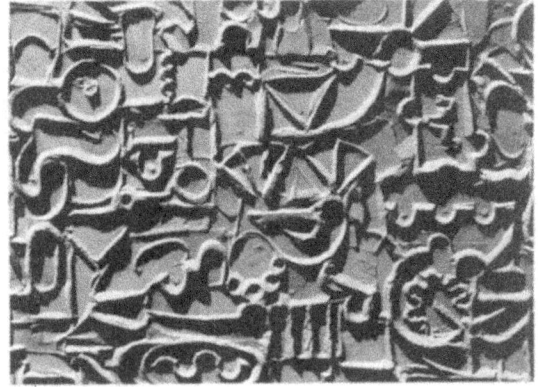

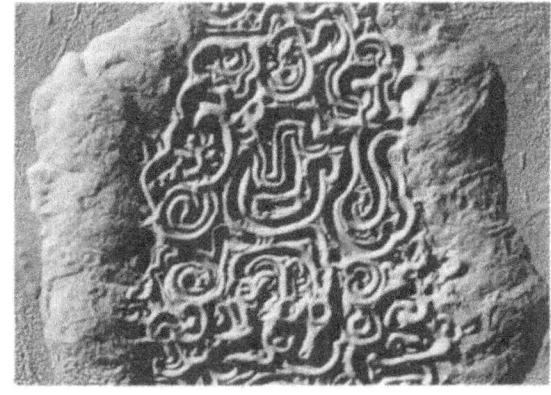

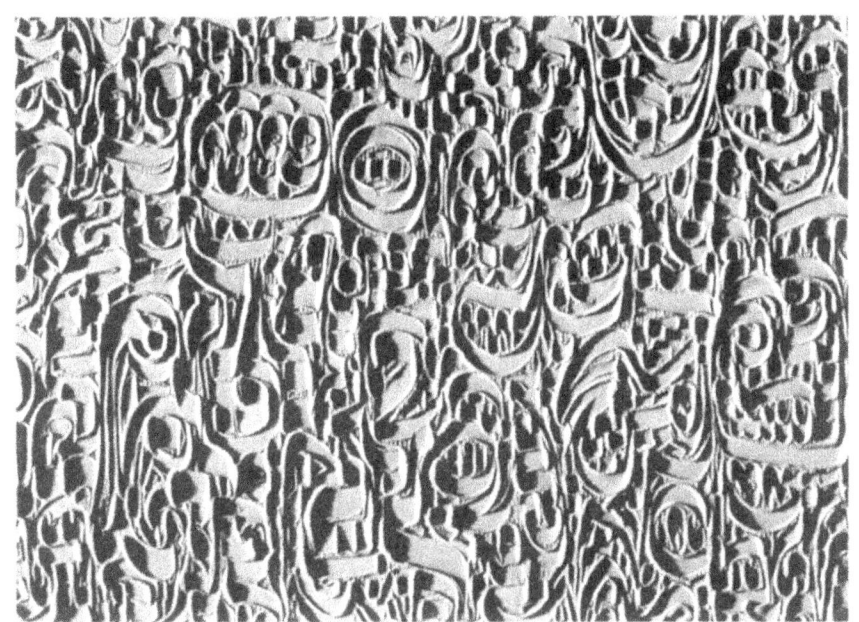

CXXVI Calligraphy

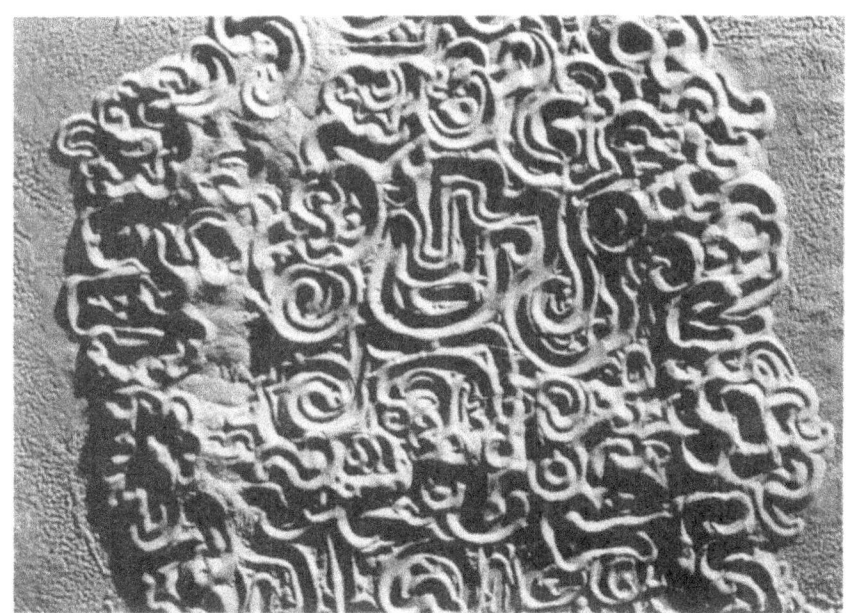

CXXVII

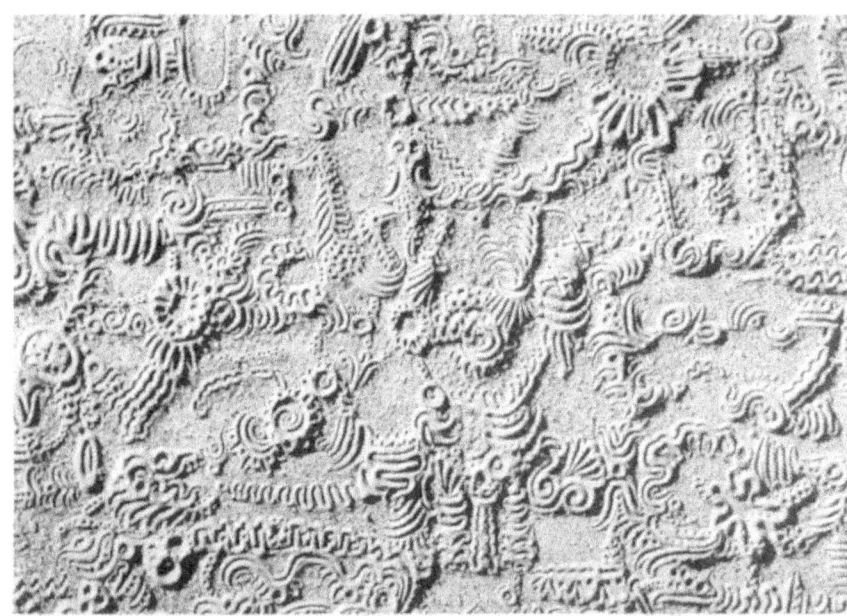

CXXVIII

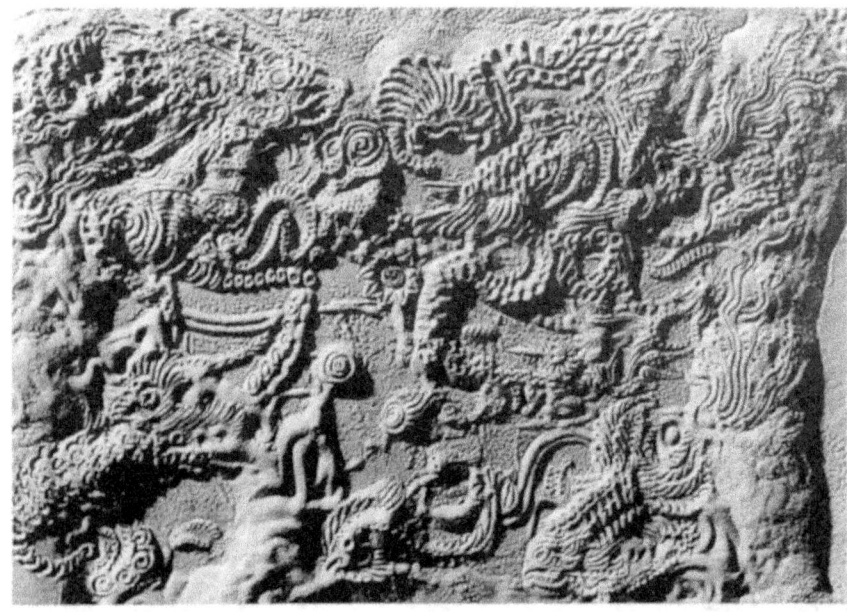

CXXIX Aquarium

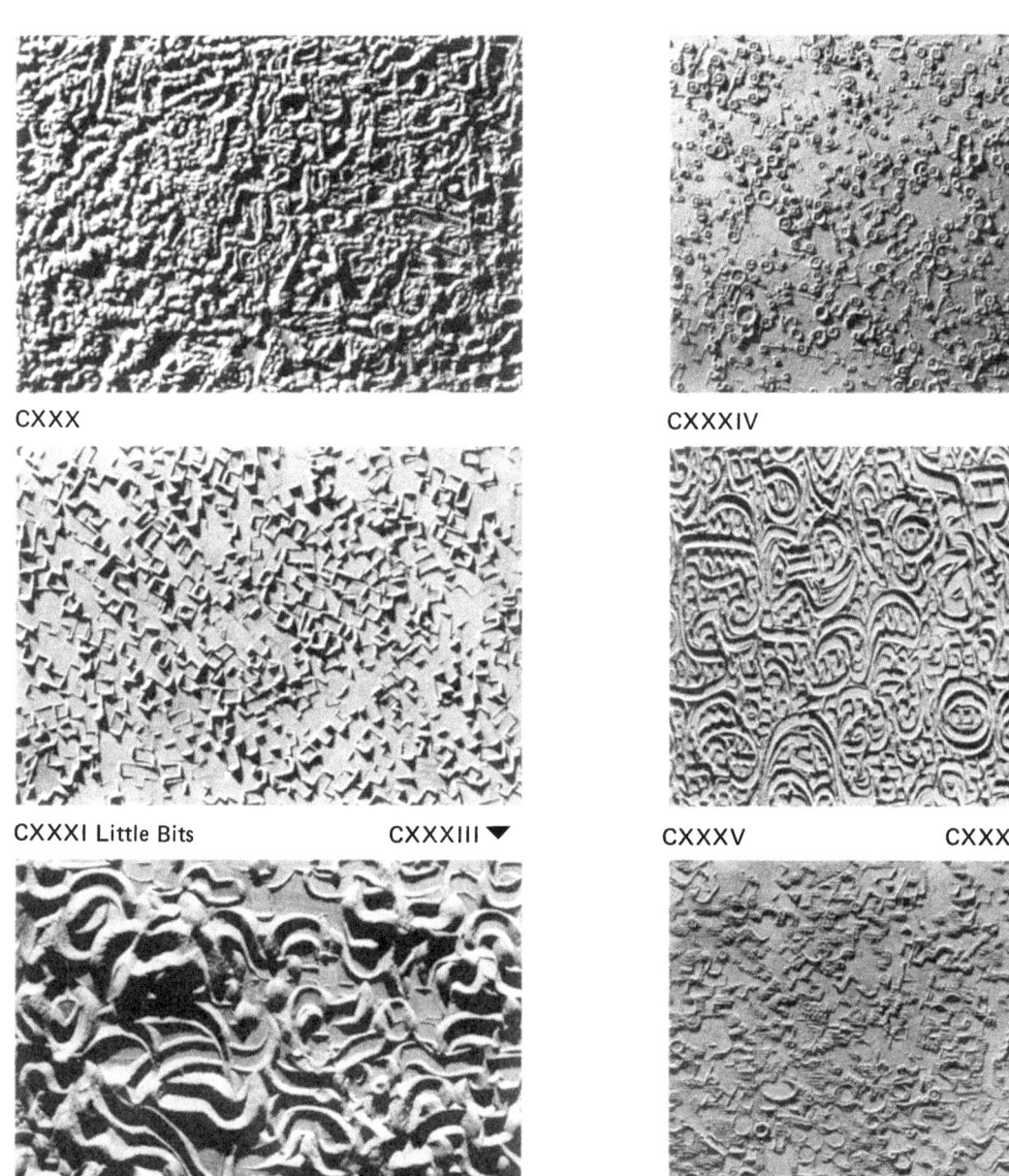

CXXX

CXXXIV

CXXXI Little Bits   CXXXIII ▼

CXXXV   CXXXVI Trinkets ▼

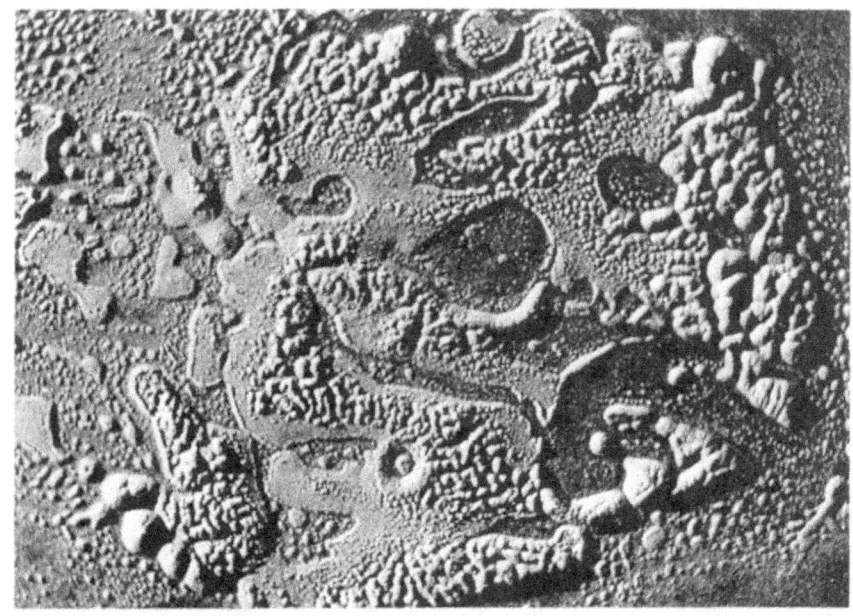

CXXXVIII Ferment

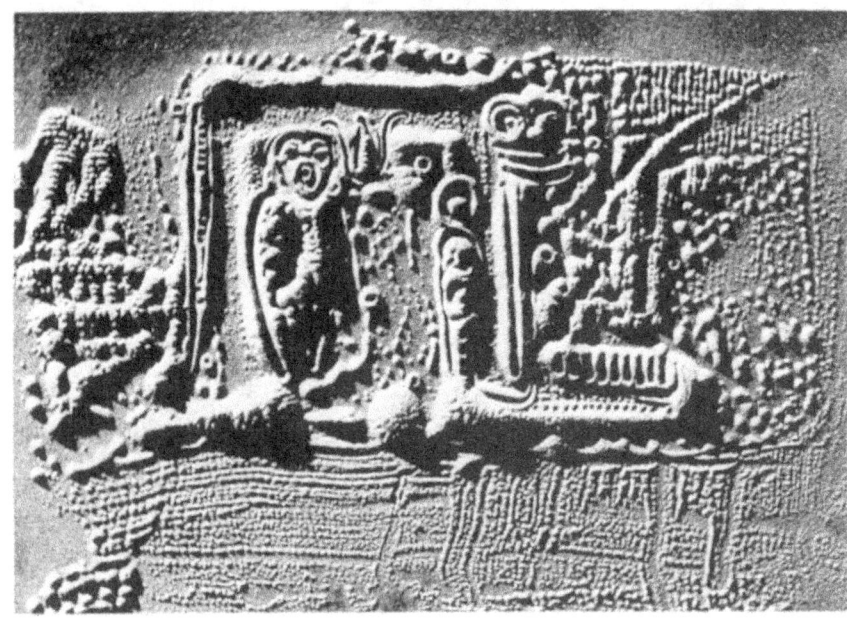

CXXXIX

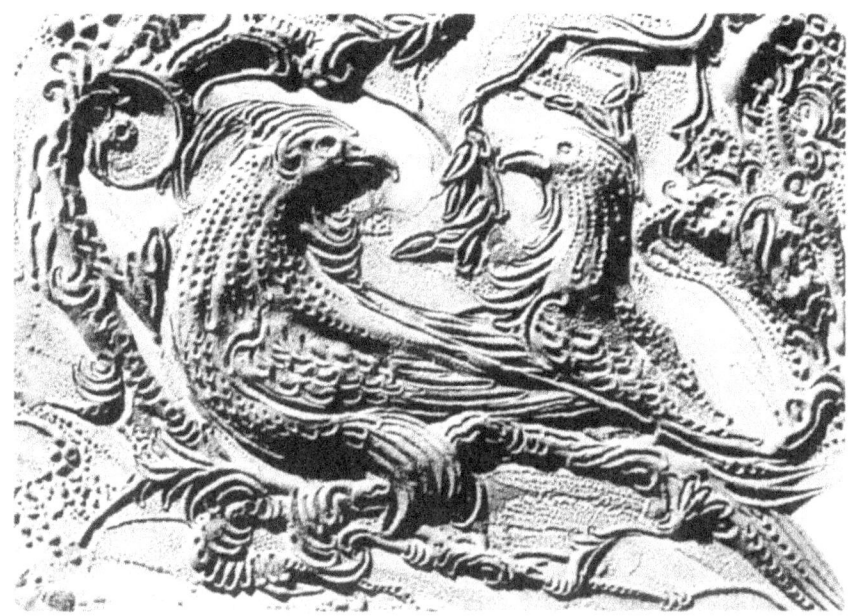

CXL Two Birds

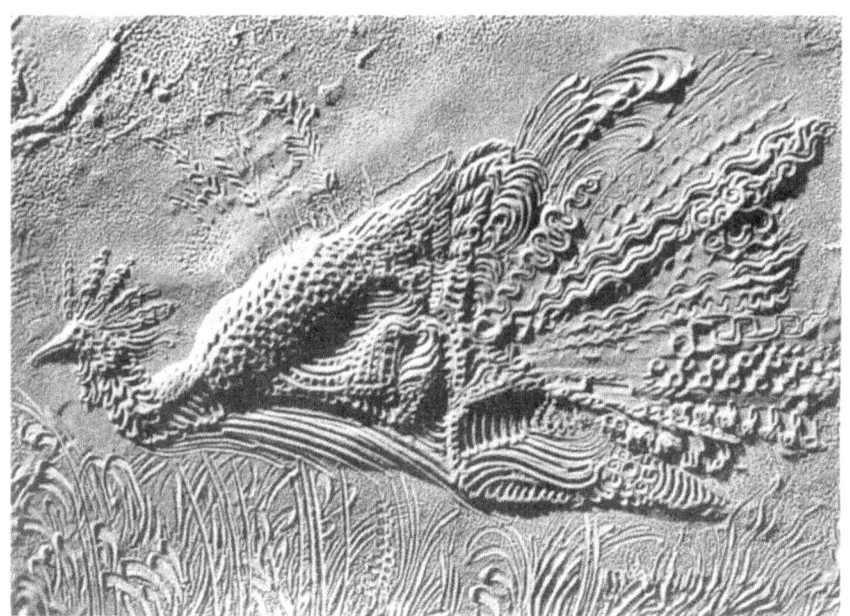

CXLI Phoenix

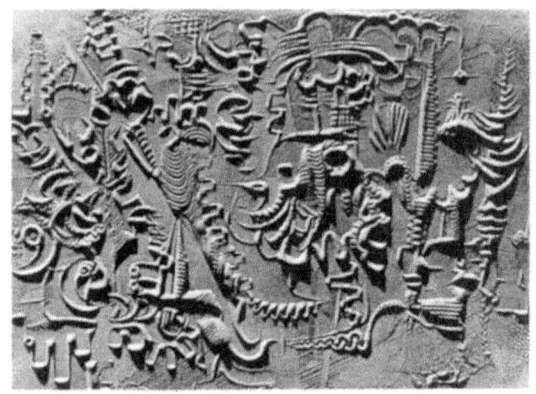

CXLII Jewels

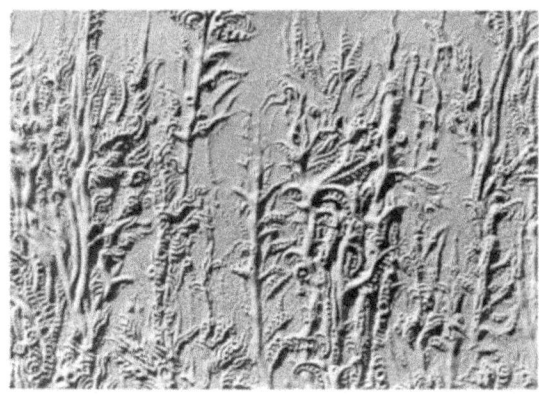

CXLV

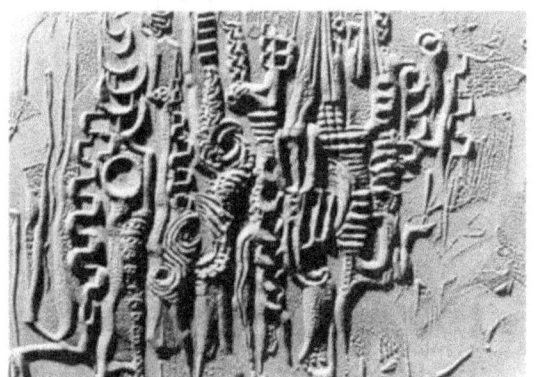

CXLIII Trophies   CXLIV Fern ▼

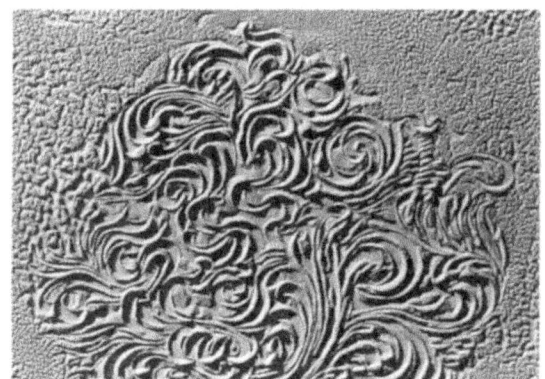

CXLVI   CXLVII Rooster ▼

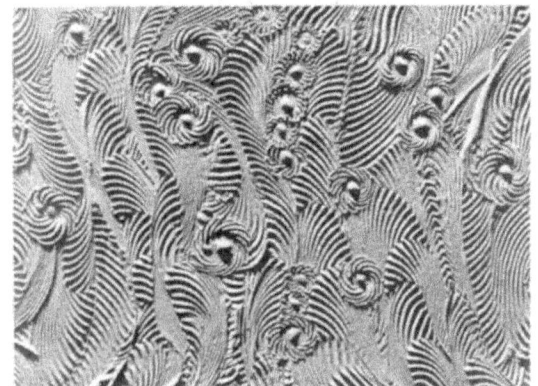

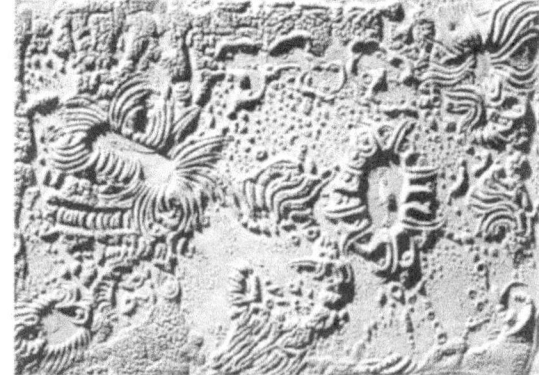

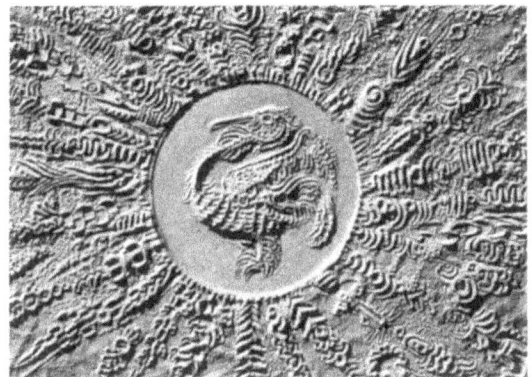

CXLVIII

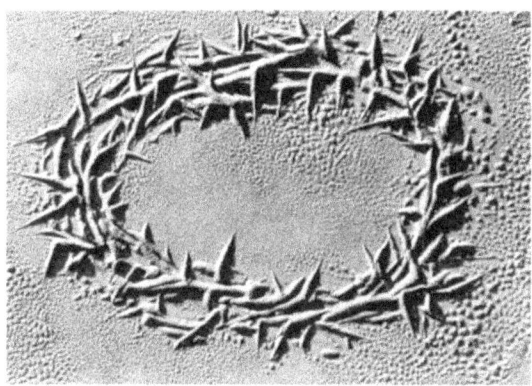

CLI Crown of Thorns

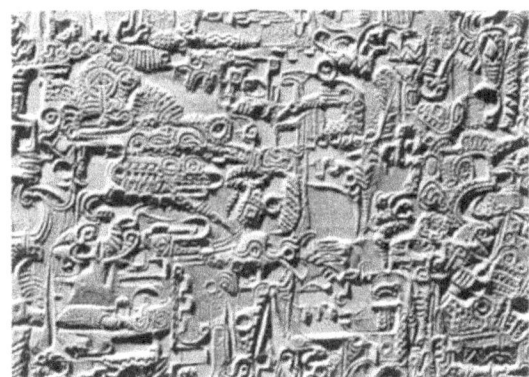

CXLIX Scribble
CL Bark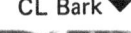

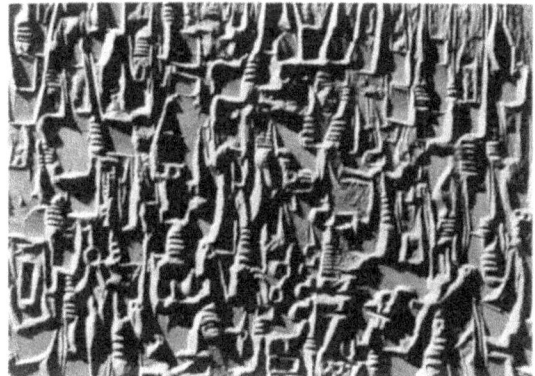

CLII
CLIII ▼

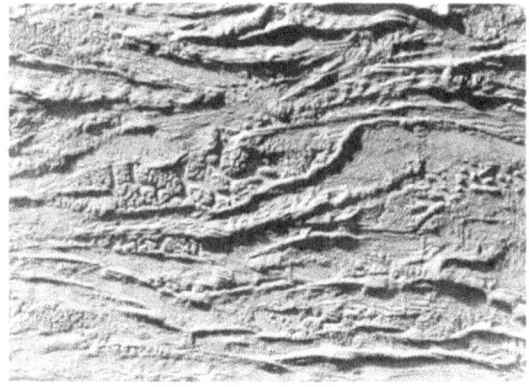

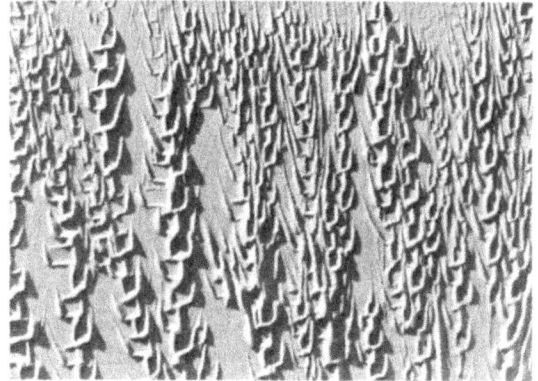

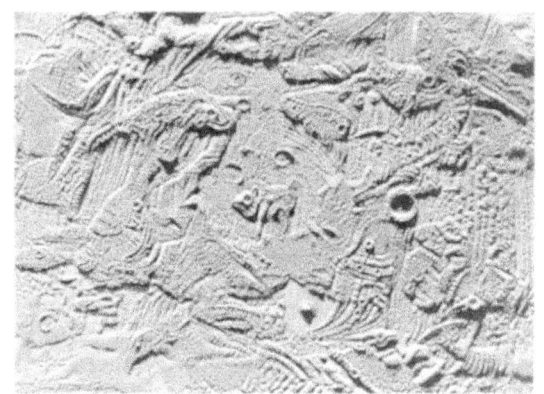

CLIV Puppy

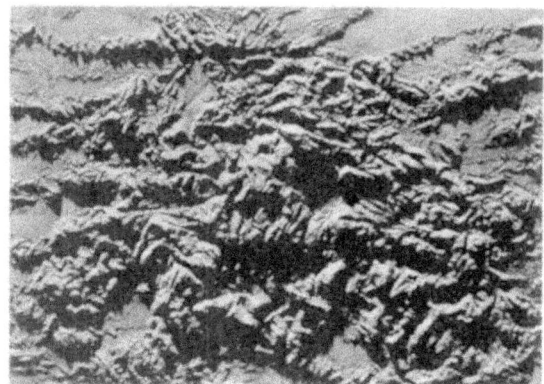

CLIX Rough Terrain

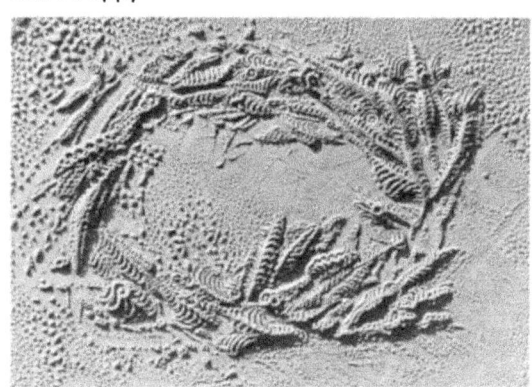

CLVI   CLVII ▼

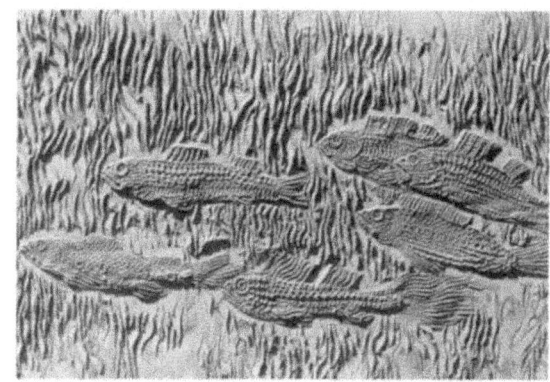

CLX Fish   CLXI ▼

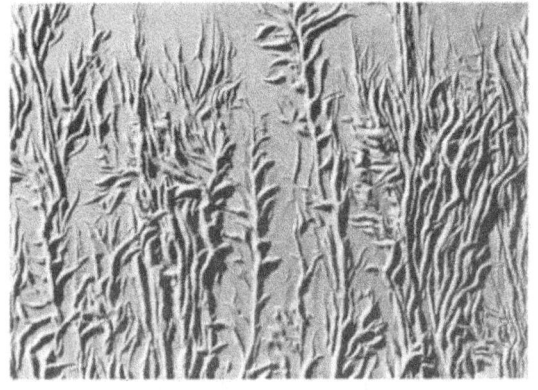

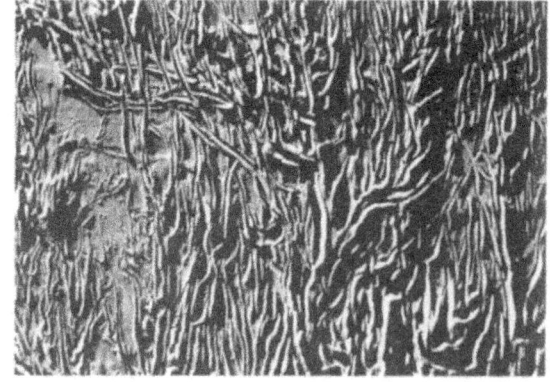

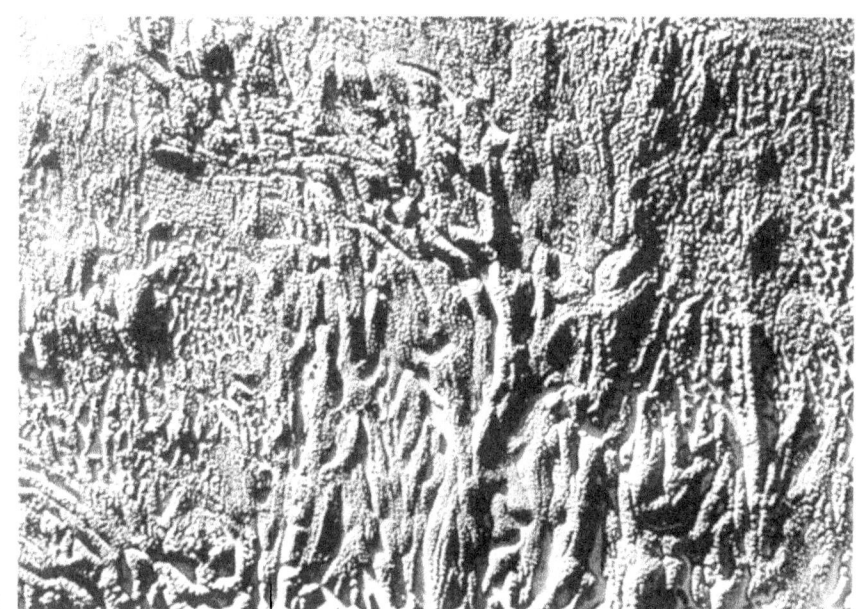

CLXIII

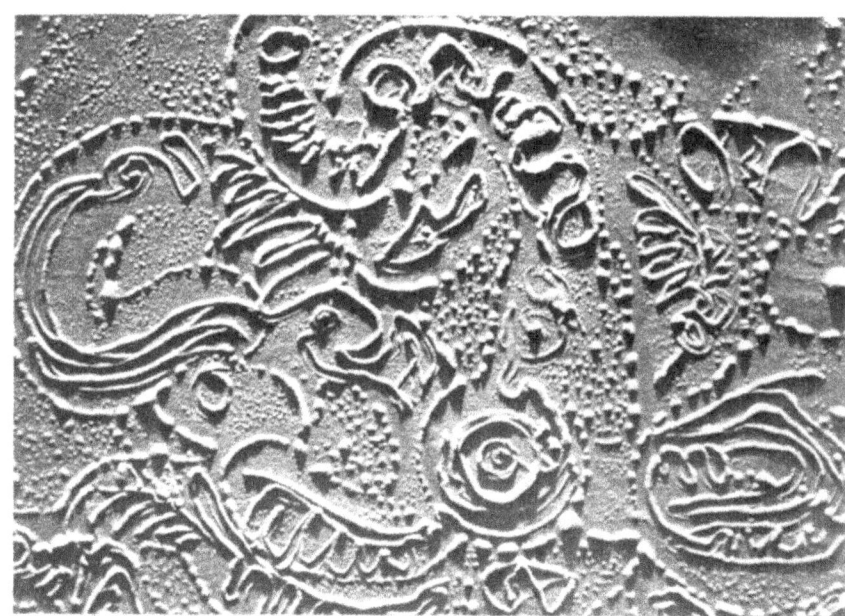

CLXIV

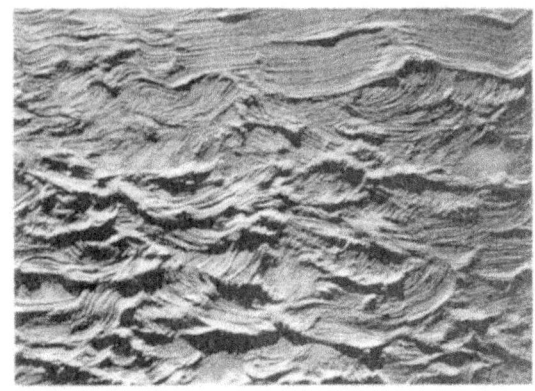

CLXVIII

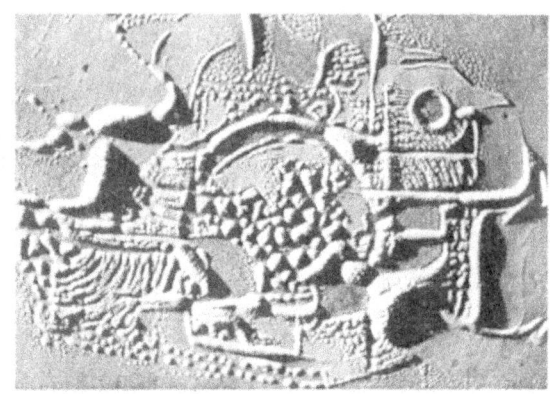

CLXXVI

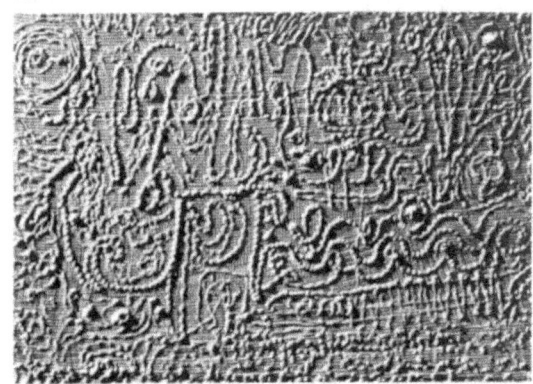

CLXX   CLXXIV ▼

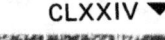

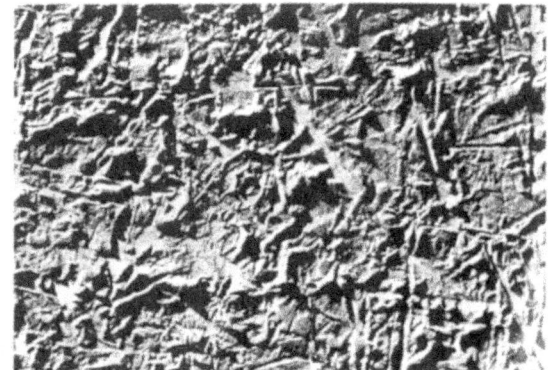

CLXXVII   CLXXVIII ▼

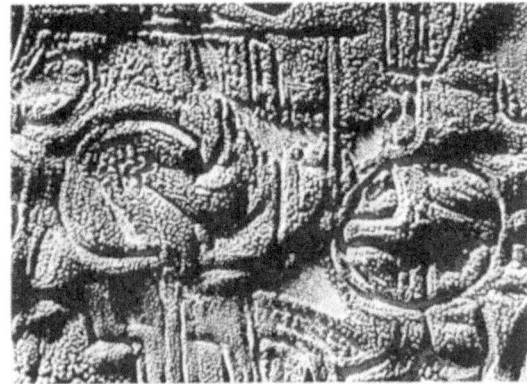

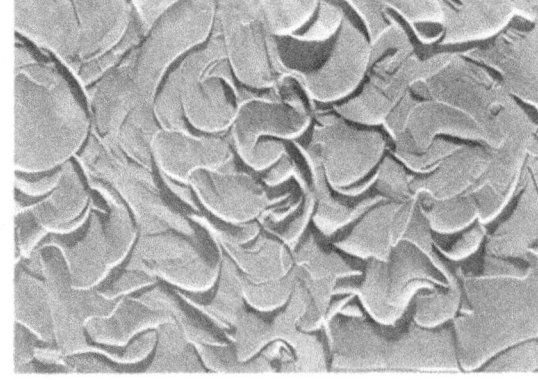

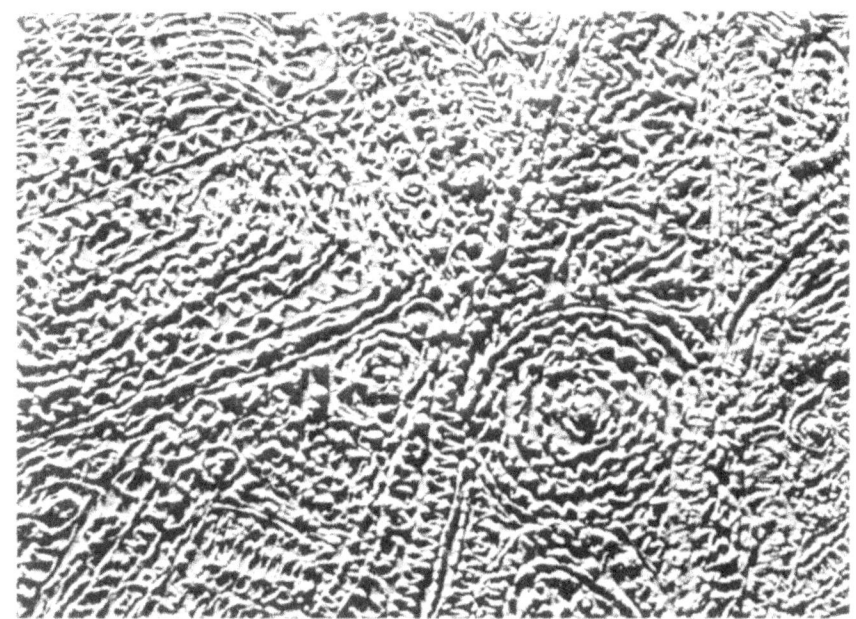

CLXXIX

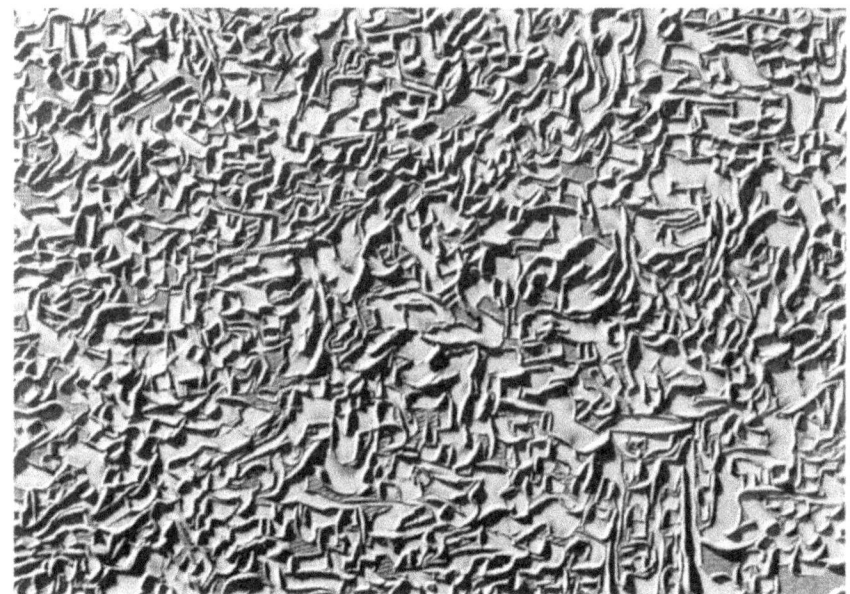

CLXXX

Images in Sand
was composed and printed
at the University of Kentucky
Department of Printing Services
and bound by the C. J. Krehbiel Company
of Cincinnati, Ohio.

Design by Robert James Foose

www.ingramcontent.com/pod-product-compliance
Lightning Source LLC
Chambersburg PA
CBHW080931170526
45158CB00008B/2253